John Mullins

Free libraries and newsrooms

Their formation and management

John Mullins

Free libraries and newsrooms
Their formation and management

ISBN/EAN: 9783337283537

Printed in Europe, USA, Canada, Australia, Japan

Cover: Foto ©Suzi / pixelio.de

More available books at **www.hansebooks.com**

FREE LIBRARIES

AND

NEWSROOMS:

THEIR

FORMATION AND MANAGEMENT.

BY

J. D. MULLINS,

CHIEF LIBRARIAN BIRMINGHAM FREE LIBRARIES.

[Read at the Meeting of the National Association for the Promotion
of Social Science at Birmingham, 1868.]

Third Edition.

WITH CONSIDERABLE ADDITIONS.

LONDON:

HENRY SOTHERAN AND CO., 36, PICCADILLY.

1879.

PREFACE.

The writer has for some time past been constantly receiving applications from various parts of the country for particulars as to the Formation and Management of Free Libraries. A strong desire for their extension, as well as courtesy to the persons applying, have compelled him to write various letters, giving information and advice to the best of his ability. The following pages are simply a summary of these letters. There is a great need for an able popular Manual on the subject: for this he regrets that he has neither the time nor the power. These notes are published in the hope that some more competent person may be induced to prepare a more complete and valuable guide to the foundation and management of the greatest educational machinery of our age.

SUMMARY OF CONTENTS.

NOTE.—The original Free Libraries' Act, 1850, is not reprinted here, as it is rescinded.

Free Libraries and Newsrooms.

For many years the United Kingdom has possessed in its various divisions Libraries easy of access to men of taste and learning. Some few of these have been called Free Libraries; that is to say, no money has been taken for admission to them, but usually some such introduction or recommendation has been required as has served as a barrier to the common people, and indeed to all but very earnest and persevering students. Other Libraries have been accessible on terms of subscription apparently suitable to all _lasses, but on an inquiry as to the number and condition of the persons using all the Literary Institutions known, it was found that they formed but a marvellously small part of the population, and that the great mass of the people, who stood most in need of information, were not reached.

Some men thought that there was nothing to be done in such a case but to leave ill alone, especially as interference meant expense. To others it appeared that wholesome reading and thought made much of the difference between the brutish and mischievous and the intelligent and useful of mankind; and that it might really be the truest thrift, as well as the noblest generosity, to carry the pleasures of learning and the influence of literature to those who did not care to come to them. It was thought to be not unlikely that what was spent on Free Libraries and Newsrooms might be saved in Workhouses and Gaols; and so the experiment was tried. The people had been mourned over and denounced for haunting this and that improper place for recreation—de-

1

nounced and mourned over in vain—until it occurred to some one that perhaps it might be worth while to provide something pleasant and good as a counter-attraction. The jaded merchant, the harassed tradesman, and the tired student, usually have the grateful change of pleasant homes, the various resources of society, of art, of music, and the like ; the poorer classes, with similar capacity for pleasure, have no such provision ; there are very seldom quiet rooms at home where they can read, even if they could get acceptable books.

Attempts to found and support Free Libraries by subscription have been made, but have met with little success. Such movements have had the brand of charity upon them, which has been to many an insuperable hindrance to their use. They have usually been sustained, too, by a party ; and the style of the books and periodicals provided has been too often eminently parochial. The clergy and gentry of the neighbourhood have kindly given such books of their own as they did not particularly care to keep, and with a few purchases of works " proper for working people," the Library has consisted of the " Life of Colonel Gardiner," Doddridge's " Rise and Progress," " Alleine's " Alarm," the " Anxious Enquirer," the " Dairyman's Daughter," Pinnock's Catechisms, some volumes of the " Mother's Magazine," a few " Annual Registers," and a choice collection of funeral sermons. Now, without for one moment disparaging the excellent works named, or the class of which they are typical, it is really no wonder that Libraries of the kind described, kept in some church or chapel schoolroom by an occasional Librarian, have not been largely used. Let it be distinctly understood that no sneer is here intended at the kindly efforts which have been made to found Parish Libraries ; but their promoters have admitted that they have been used rather by the better class of their people, who, having books, etc., of their own, could have done very well without the Library, and have failed to attract, to any considerable extent, the persons for whom they were specially intended.

There are some very noble traits in the character of the

rough working Englishman. He cannot go to, nor use, any Newsroom or Library in connection with a church or chapel, without feeling that it pledges him more or less to being religious. Now the mass of labouring men are not what is called religious; but they hold to an unconscious paraphrase of religion in what they call fairness—to work fair, to speak fair, even to fight fair, is their version of righteousness; and with all our faults, the last thing that occurs to a healthy Englishman is to play the hypocrite, or pretend to be religious for any purpose whatever.

With the history of Free Libraries, established by Corporations and supported by rates, the name of William Ewart is inseparably connected. His motion in 1848 for a Parliamentary Committee on Public Libraries led to an exposure of the deficiencies of this country, even as compared with others; of the need for an ampler supply of books, and for easier access to the Libraries containing them. Much very curious and interesting information may be gathered from the Report issued by this Committee, and from the valuable History of Libraries, by Edwards. For our purpose at present, it is enough to say that Mr. Ewart followed up his first success by obtaining the various Acts and Amendments on Libraries from 1850 to 1867.[*]

To Manchester belongs the honour of first adopting the Act, and to Manchester certainly credit is due for the most extended use and most thorough organization of these Institutions. It should be stated in praise of her citizens that they have not only granted the full allowance of one penny in the pound of their rates, but have supplemented the same with magnificent gifts. At Liverpool even more handsome donations have been given, in addition to the rates; the costly structure which contains the Library and Museum being the present of one of her grateful sons. In Birmingham the Corporation has spent nearly thirty thousand pounds in building and furnishing, and spends five thousand per annum in maintaining her Libraries and Newsrooms. Here all seems

---

[*] See also Acts for 1871, &c., in Appendix I.

to have been done by the Corporation alone. While the town is, and well may be proud of these institutions, either from lack of means or opportunity none of the merchants or gentry seemed to have helped in the work as in the other places named.

There are also Free Libraries at Airdrie, Blackburn, Bolton, Cambridge, Cardiff, Coventry, Dundee, Leamington, Norwich, Nottingham, Oxford, Salford, Sheffield, and Walsall.*

How are these Institutions worked; and how are they used?

THE NEWSROOM.

First, the Newsrooms. These are essential. They are the first step of the ladder. With the mass of men the practice of reading commences with the Newspaper and the Periodical. Now it is not fair to assume that the only purpose the News-room serves is to keep men posted up in the latest style of murder or the newest form of swindling. The various questions of the day—political, social, and moral—are in the various papers discussed by able men from their different points of view; and the reading of these articles must induce thought, tend to lessen conceit and ignorance, and lead to sound judgment. The opinion of a man of one newspaper —who gets all his information from one side—is not worth much.

* This was in 1868, but since the first edition of this pamphlet was issued, many more Free Libraries have been established, and the list now stands :—Aberystwith, Airdrie, Ashton-under-Lyne, Bebington, Bilston (Staffordshire), Birkenhead, Birmingham, Blackburn, Bolton, Bradford (Yorkshire), Bridgewater, Brighton, Bristol, Burslem, Cambridge, Canterbury, Cardiff, Carlisle, Chester, Chesterfield, Coventry, Derby, Devon and Exeter, Doncaster, Dudley, Dundalk, Dundee, Ennis, Forfar, Glasgow, Hereford, Hertford, Ipswich, Kidderminster, Leamington, Leeds, Leicester, Lichfield, Liverpool, London (Guildhall), Lynn, Macclesfield, Maidstone, Manchester, Middlesborough, Newcastle-on-Tyne, Newport, Mon., Northampton, Norwich, Nottingham, Oxford, Paisley, Penzance, Plymouth, Preston, Reading, Rochdale, Salford, Sheffield, Southport, South Shields, Stafford, Stirling, Stockport, Stoke-upon-Trent, Stockton-on-Tees, Swansea, Sunderland, Tynemouth, Walsall, Warrington, Warwick. Wednesbury, West Bromwich, Westminster, Wigan, Willenhall, Winchester, Wolverhampton, Wrexham.

Take a day in these Newsrooms. They open at nine in the morning; by this time there is a crowd of men and lads round the door—artisans, clerks, labourers, many of them out of employ, waiting to see the advertisements. The Newsroom either helps them to work or serves as a resource in the weary hours of waiting—a resource cheaper, and in other respects much better, than the tavern. A little later, with the London papers, comes another class—tradesmen and persons of small income, to whom a pound or other subscription to a Newsroom would be out of the question, but who take the two or three shillings per annum they pay in rates out in reading for themselves and families, which certainly does them no harm; nay, they enrich themselves at very little cost, and yet leave abundant provision for poorer men behind; for it should always be remembered in dealing with this matter, that the Library rate is not like the Poor rate and some other taxes, illimitable: it cannot go beyond one penny in the pound, so that each ratepayer can estimate exactly what it will cost him, and judge whether the expense is serious enough to justify opposition to a movement that has resulted in benefit wherever it has been permitted. At mid-day the working men crowd in again, giving half the dinner hour to the mind. All day long the rooms are well used, and at night are crowded. Men who otherwise would confine their reading to the Police News, or murder made easy, and similar garbage, get the best of the current literature. The one room in view is used by more than two thousand men daily; multiply these rooms and the result is incalculable.* The charm of the place is its absolute freedom. While it is used most largely by the poorer classes, yet many of the prosperous are there as well. There is perfect equality, no favour, and no jealousy; and though used chiefly by the comparatively un-

---

* In several towns the rooms used in the day time as Board Schools are used at night as Public Newsrooms. This is a comparatively inexpensive mode of meeting a great want, and the only objection seems to be that it is likely to injure the business of the small beerhouses.

educated, the order and quietness of the place cannot be surpassed. The Room is handsome, lofty, and well furnished. It is remarked that the men in corduroy are treated as gentlemen, and they behave as such. It is quite possible that a barn in a back-slum would not be so successful; if gin-palaces and the like are brilliant and handsome, why should the opposition be enamoured of the dingy and the mean? Provide your free Newsroom in a good thoroughfare, let it be its own invitation, keep it open till ten at night, and it will do more to close objectionable places and break vicious habits than any number of police. In providing the newspapers and periodicals be liberal; all, or as many of the following as you can afford, will be acceptable:—**Daily**—Times, Pall Mall Gazette, Daily News, Standard, Daily Telegraph; and the Local Papers of course. **Weekly**—Academy, All the Year Round, Army and Navy Gazette, Athenæum, Australasian, Builder, Chambers's Journal, Civil Service Gazette, Dublin Freeman, Economist, Engineer, Engineering, Examiner, Fun, Gardener's Chronicle, Harper's Weekly (American), Illustrated London News, Illustrated Times, Graphic, Pictorial World, Mechanic's Magazine, Mining Journal, Notes and Queries, Once a Week, Punch, Public Opinion, Saturday Review, Scientific American, Scotsman, Spectator. **Monthly** —Argosy, Art Journal, Belgravia, Blackwood's Magazine, Cassell's Magazine, Cornhill Magazine, Contemporary Review, Fortnightly Review, Fraser's Magazine, Gentleman's Magazine, Good Words, Leisure Hour, London Society, Macmillan's Magazine, Nature, Nineteenth Century, Philosophical Magazine, Scribner's Monthly. **Quarterly** — Bibliotheca Sacra, British Quarterly Review, Dublin Review, Edinburgh Review, Journal of the Geological Society, Journal of Microscopical Science, London Quarterly Review, Popular Science Review, Quarterly Review, Journal of the Statistical Society, and Westminster Review.

Beware, unless your funds are very ample, of introducing denominational papers. You may innocently commence with the Guardian, and find, as the result, that the Record, the

Church and State Review, the Nonconformist, the Tablet, the Watchman, the Wesleyan Times, and other representative papers will be required, even to the Millennial Star and the Pot of Manna. It does *not* follow because you do not supply professedly religious papers that what you do supply is irreligious. We have now to a very large extent what Dr. Arnold said was the want of his day—not so much articles on religious subjects as articles on common subjects with a decidedly Christian tone. The periodical and newspaper literature of to-day is in this respect a great improvement on the past, and may fairly be rejoiced over. The Christianity that used to be confined to churches and conventicles now runs down our streets, and while it is none the worse for fresh air, the streets are all the better for its presence.

THE LENDING LIBRARY.

In the same Newsroom which we have been describing is carried on the *Lending Library*. From ten in the morning till nine at night persons of all classes pass in and out to borrow, return, or exchange Books, the issue reaching a thousand volumes daily ; a fair proportion being Theology, Philosophy, History, Travel, Art and Science, to a majority of works in Poetry, Fiction, etc.*

Well, yes, Fiction, though all the statistics unduly exaggerate this feature ; for the mass of books in History, Art,

---

* In a paper read at the " Conference of Librarians," by Mr. P. Cowell, of Liverpool, he mentioned the case of a poor woman who came frequently to the Lending Library to change books, and on one occasion when there was some difficulty in getting just what she wanted, begged very hard for a book, telling the Librarian confidentially that she wanted it for her husband ; for, said she, " if I have the house pleasant and a cheerful book for him to read, he stops at home of an evening with me and the children;" she did not go on to say what it meant to her if he had to go to the public-house to spend the evening, how late he came home or in what condition, but much was implied.

etc., are in one volume, while the mass of novels are in three volumes; so that the issue of one thousand works in Fiction appears by the side of the issue of one thousand others magnified to three times its real size. But taking it at its worst, is it so very serious, after all, that a man who works hard and has plenty of care should be privileged to forget it all for a few hours while on a journey with Swift to Lilliput, with Kingsley Westward Ho! with the Dodd Family Abroad, with Thackeray, or in Dickens-land? If the Library did nothing else than give an occasional hour of relief and pleasure to those who have but little of it, it would have done a good work. But it does much more than this.—The highest class of reading is well in demand; Chaucer, Spenser, Shakespeare, Milton, Locke, Newton, Jeremy Taylor, Dugald Stewart, Robert Hall, Hallam, Macaulay, Carlyle, are rapidly becoming known in a new world—a world they never thought to reach. A blacksmith asks for Euclid, and a butcher complains that the Odyssey is always out. The lads go in for Cooper and Scott and Tom Brown, and keep up a strong demand for Natural History, and the Battles of the British Army and Navy. Austen, Edgeworth, Bremer, and others wait on the lasses: while Mary Howitt and Hans Christian Andersen light up many a dark home and sad young life with glimpses of other worlds and better things.

In the formation of *Lending Libraries* it is not necessary or desirable to provide expensive works. These, if bought or given, should be kept for the *Reference Department*. If taken home and injured in any way the cost of replacing would make the Library a trouble to the borrower or to his guarantor. A collection of books suitable in every way and for all classes may be obtained at an average cost of half-a-crown a volume; get Constable's Miscellany, 82 vols.; Lardner's Cabinet Cyclopædia, 132 vols; Murray's Family Library, 80 vols.; the Traveller's. Library, 60 vols.; the Library of Entertaining Knowledge, 43 vols.: the Edinburgh Cabinet Library, 38 vols.; Jardine's Naturalist's Library, 40 vols.; Johnson's Poets, 75 vols.; Nichol's Poets,

42 vols.; Chambers's Tracts, 20 vols.; Select Library of Fiction, 132 vols.; Knight's Weekly Volumes, 95 parts; Bohn's Antiquarian, Ecclesiastical, Historical, Illustrated, Standard, and other Libraries; Weale's Scientific and Educational Series; cheap editions of the writings of Guthrie, F. W. Robertson, Caird, Stanley, Mill, Hume, Gibbon, Goldsmith, Macaulay, Carlyle, Hugh Miller, Austen, Scott, Cooper, James, Dickens, etc. Have sets of the Periodicals—Chambers's Journal, Household Words, All the Year Round, Good Words, Leisure Hour, Once a Week, and the like.* Have, as your means will allow, the cheap popular manuals on Astronomy, Botany, Chemistry, Geology, etc., and you have a Library good enough for a prince, and none too good for your working man. It will occur to an outsider that the sets of Constable, Lardner, etc. are somewhat too old for a modern Library; but it will be found that though a little old they are by no means obsolete, but still contain the best and in many cases the only good concise works on the subjects of which they treat. They are essential for both the *Reference* and *Lending Libraries.* It is found that as a rule the books are taken remarkable care of, and that if damaged or lost they are willingly paid for or replaced. At Birmingham, out of an issue of 300,000 volumes in one year, only 20 volumes were lost.

REFERENCE LIBRARY.

There is yet another department to notice—the *Reference Library.* This is not merely a place for dictionaries, atlases, and so on, although, of course, it contains them; but is called the " Reference Library " because the books in it may not be taken away, but must be used on the premises. To many persons, as we have said, a quiet place to read in is more difficult to obtain than books to read. Hence, this department is largely used. Choice and costly works on the Fine Arts, on Design, on Ornament, on Colour, on Architec-

* An extended list of desirable Books will be found in Appendix V.

ture, on Mechanics, Engineering, and the various Sciences are here; and the artisan or mechanic can and does study these and gets quietly the technical education so much talked of. History, Travel, Nature, Law, Poetry, Theology, are here magnificently illustrated, and their lessons gladly learned.

It seems impossible to visit these places and see how they are used without expressions of surprise at their success and of enthusiasm in their favour. Booksellers, who feared that they would injure their trade, find that they create a taste for reading, and multiply their customers. Subscription Libraries find that the Free Libraries, so far from injuring them, serve as pioneers for them. Persons begin to read when they can get the books for nothing; the taste once created, they willingly pay for its gratification.

Presuming that every considerable town in the kingdom will sooner or later adopt an Act bringing in such advantages, an outline of the methods generally pursued in the formation of such Institutions may be useful. The initiative is seldom taken by the Town Council, or governing body, the members not being usually as alive to their privileges in this respect as could be wished. To apprehend and provide for the needs of the people under their care is specially the province of the local government, and when it fails to do this, it neglects the exercise of its noblest powers. Supposing the local government to suffer either from timidity or inertia, or to be under the control of persons who make it their business to stifle all that is generous with the rag of pseudo-economy, the custom is to call together the ministers of religion, the teachers of the Sunday and night schools, and all other persons who desire the well-being and improvement of their fellows; these, after discussion, memorialize the Council to call the burgesses together. (See form, Appendix III.) Meanwhile, they collect reports from the various towns having Free Libraries, and publish selections from these reports in the local newspapers and in handbills. Soothe the economists by showing them how very little it will cost them per head; and get round the gentleman who says he never reads books—and has lived all his life without Libraries and Newsrooms—and look at him! They get all the philanthropy and eloquence and truth they can bring to bear on the subject to the meeting, or they fail to get a majority. The natural resistance to new things, especially if they are good, is always strong; and carelessness or too much confidence will lose the day. In no place has the Act been adopted without much preparation and enlightenment through the concert of good and determined men : the Act has been rejected in several places through premature or too hasty action; but where it has once been adopted, it has never been repented of or rescinded.

On the adoption of the Act by the Burgesses, the governing body will appropriate,—according as it is generous or otherwise, — a halfpenny or a penny in the pound of its income to the purposes of the Act. It is only fair to say that usually when the Act has once been adopted, the Town Council, seeing that the thing has to be done, has decided to do it handsomely, and the whole rate has been granted. Then a Committee, consisting half of its own members and half of the scholarly men of the neighbourhood, has been appointed, and permission has been given to borrow money for building on the security of the rate, such money to be paid off by instalments out of the yearly income.

As to the Building. To open with a poor building with a bad entrance in a back street is not the way to ensure success. To get and try to fit-up a private house for the purpose is very likely to be money wasted. A really good site in a populous thoroughfare, and a building of some character and prominence, are as necessary for the success of a Library as for the success of a saloon or a gin-palace. The building should announce itself boldly to be what it is, and should be as inviting and appear as pleasant as the places it is intended to supersede. A handsome entrance well lighted, with a passage between the entrance and the Reading Room as long as you can get, so as to keep the room quiet; the room itself should be spacious lofty and well ventilated, lighted from the roof if a one-story building, or if an upper room, and if a lower room lighted by windows from six to eight feet from the ground, so as to avoid the disturbance often resulting from view of the street, and also to secure handy wall-space for book-shelves, maps, pictures, and the like. As to the number of rooms, the more rooms, the more difficult the task of oversight, and the greater the number of assistants required. To erect a building of many rooms or several stories, put a Museum in one, a Library in another, and a Newsroom in a third, and to set one man to look after the whole, is not wise, as he will often be required in the three places at once. Have as many rooms as you please, if you can place an officer or two in each; but as the majority of places which have yet to form Libraries, etc., will have but moderate means, it is worth while to try and point out how to make the most of these. There seems to be no great difficulty in having one good room a Newsroom, Lending and Reference Libraries, and a Museum. (*See* Plan at front.)

The borrowers of books, boys, messengers, etc., on this plan only just enter the ante-chamber of the building, and get served; the readers on the premises pass on into a quieter part, and pursue their studies undisturbed; while the whole is under the eye of the Librarian. The floor should be matted, and quietness and cleanliness be very firmly but civilly enforced. Let your officers be well-bred men and youths; have no flashy young swells who will treat the poorer borrowers as if they were paupers. Let them understand that there is to be no respect of persons; if additional courtesy and favour are to be shown anywhere they should be to the poorest. There is a power in a fair and courteous administration that is irresistible. If to knowledge, courtesy and firmness, your Librarian can add a sympathy with the men who need information, and a pride in helping them, he will fill a very happy office, and his Library will be a great success.

THE LIBRARY CATALOGUE.

The mass of borrowers at the Lending Libraries will be poor people; the Library will be of little use to them without a Catalogue. This must be had for a few pence or they will not buy it; it must be simple or they will not be able to use it. The following method has been found to work well:—
Divide the books into classes, thus—

A. THEOLOGY and PHILOSOPHY.
B. BIOGRAPHY.
C. HISTORY and TRAVELS.
D. LAW, POLITICS, and POLITICAL ECONOMY.
E. NATURAL HISTORY.
F. ARTS and SCIENCES.
G. POETRY and the DRAMA.
H. FICTION.
I. MISCELLANEOUS.
J. JUVENILE BOOKS.

Brevity is necessary to cheapness; hence you enter each work but once, and then by the word under which it is most likely to be looked for.

In Theology and Philosophy the name of the author is more important than the subject; hence the A Section is catalogued by itself, and of course alphabetically under the author where the author is given; and where there is no author, under the title, as—

Guthrie (J.) Speaking to the Heart . 21 A
Heaven our Home . . . . 85 A

In Biography, History, Voyages and Travels, the subject of the Biography, and the country or place written of, are specially the subjects of inquiry; hence these sections should be catalogued under their subjects. In Law, Politics, and Political Economy, the authors prevail. In Arts, Sciences, and Natural History, the subject. In Fiction, Poetry, etc., the

author is uppermost again.   A specimen of a catalogue after
this fashion is appended :—

ALEXANDER the Great, Life of, by Williams   .   .   .   1 B
Ali Pasha, Life of, by Davenport   .   .   .   .   .   .   2 B
Anne Boleyn, Memoirs of, by Benger   .   .   .   .   .   202 B
Anson (Lord) Life of, by Barrow   .   .   .   .   .   200 B
Apostles, Lives of the, by Cave .   .   .   .   .   .   44 B
Bacon (Lord) Life of, by Dixon   .   .   .   .   .   .   370 B
Bedell (W.) Life of, by Hone   .   .   .   .   .   .   25 B
Biography of Converts from Christianity, by Crichton   .   .   52 B
Biography of British Painters, Sculptors, and Architects, by
    A. Cunningham   .   .   .   .   114 B

> Vol. 1.—Hogarth. Wilson. Reynolds. Gainsborough.
> Vol. 2.—West. Blake. Opie. Morland. Bird. Fuseli. Barry.
> Vol. 3.—Gibbons. Roubillac. Wilton. Banks. Nollekens.
> Vol. 4.—Wykeham. Jones. Wren. Vanbrugh. Gibbs. Kent. Burlington.
>   Chambers.
> Vol. 5.—Jamesone. Ramsay. Romney. Runciman. Copley. Mortimer. Racburn.
>   Hopner. Owen. Harlow. Bonington.
> Vol. 6.—Cosway. Allan. Northcote. Beaumont. Lawrence. Jackson. Liver-
>   seege. Burnet.

Biography, Footprints of Famous Men, by Edgar   .   .   .   15 B

Printed like it in Brevier and Nonpareil, and in double
column, a catalogue of a considerable Library may be sold for
a few pence.

For the Reference Department, where the books are more
various and costly, and the readers of a somewhat different
class, a fuller catalogue may be given.   But here the danger
is in attempting too much.   The largest and most valuable
libraries in England and on the Continent are greatly depre-
ciated, so far as usefulness is concerned, by their non-posses-
sion of printed catalogues of their works.   It is nearly
impossible to ascertain what is in them.   How greatly the
value of the Library at the British Museum would be en-
hanced to students and the general public if there existed a
printed catalogue of its contents.   The truth is that Librarians generally in their natural anxiety that the catalogue of
their Library shall be an addition to the science of criticism
and bibliography, have aimed at so elaborate a description of
each work that the catalogue never gets printed, or if printed

costs so much as to sell at a price quite out of reach of the persons frequenting Free Libraries.

It would ill become the writer to speak lightly of the valuable catalogue prepared by Dr. Crestadoro of the Manchester Reference Library, in which the entry of each work gives something like a photograph of the title-page, and adds the number of pages each work contains. All students of bibliography admire this catalogue, but few would have the courage or perseverance to imitate it. The catalogue of the Liverpool* Reference Library is a handsome volume, containing a very able classification of a fine Library; but the costliness of both these works, and the character of the latter, prevent their use to any considerable extent by the common people for whom Free Libraries are specially intended. It is possible to catalogue twenty thousand volumes in such a manner as to show the student or reader at a glance all the works by any author or on any subject wanted. Every book should be entered under its author and under its title, and again under its subject; for instance, Ruskin's *Stones of Venice* would be entered under "Ruskin," "Venice," and again under "Architecture." Waring's *Masterpieces of the Exhibition* would be entered under "Waring," "Exhibition," and again under "Art." Miller's *Testimony of the Rocks* would go under "Miller," "Testimony of the Rocks," and "Geology." Warburton's *Hochelaga* would go under "Warburton," "Hochelaga," and again under "Canada." Against these triple entries of one work are to be set the works for which one entry would suffice.

Confine the description of each work to one line, giving only the gist of the title-page and omitting its verbiage. Thus it is possible to catalogue twenty thousand volumes, which would represent about six thousand works, in a very small compass, and print the same at a very small cost.

The catalogue is in appearance a rough alphabetical list of books, but possesses in reality all the advantages of a classified catalogue without its embarrassments. A work of the kind

* Liverpool has since issued another catalogue.

will shortly be published, and then the author will probably be punished for his presumption in this matter by the exposure of its defects.*

The writer would guard against the favour which he may be supposed to have for Free Libraries from his official connection with them, and would not willingly exaggerate their importance ; but some interest in the matter may fairly be claimed when the results are so evident. Adopt any of the systems of primary education which have been so much discussed of late, and a generation must pass away before their effect can be realized. In the work of Free Libraries you may both sow and live to reap. What are called the lower classes do manage to read to themselves and to one another to a far greater extent than is supposed. It is not uncommon to see one man reading very laboriously and very badly to another man who cannot read at all. Go into the lowest quarters of any great town, and see the number of shops that exist for the sale of cheap periodical literature. These are proof enough of the demand, of the hunger and thirst for information. But what about the supply ? Here you have the " Mysteries of London," and the like, tales of villainy and seduction, thrilling romances, always being " continued in our next." Here you have the great weekly Murdermonger, four-and-twenty columns of crime and filth for one penny. Here you have the Halfpenny Holocaust, the largest paper in the world, and all on one side. And the people feed on these for want of knowing better. Turn a pure language upon them, give them a wholesome and pleasant literature, and the statistics of existing Free Libraries prove that they will both use and value it. Visit the homes of the labouring classes ; the men come home soon after five or six at night, get a wash and their tea. They cannot be expected always to stay at home and nurse the child—where shall they spend their few spare hours pleasantly ? If there are Free Newsrooms they go to them ; if not, probably to the public-house ; and who

* The catalogue referred to, was issued in 1869, and met with most kindly notice from the *Athenæum* and other reviewers.

can fairly blame them ? We must have these Free Libraries
and Newsrooms in every town. Edinburgh has, to the surprise and pain of her admirers, refused to adopt the Act,
but she will think better of it yet. Hull, Huddersfield,
Dublin, Belfast, Glasgow and Leeds,* with their large
resources ; the great divisions of London—Islington, Marylebone, Southwark—and other places have yet to decide in
favour of the Libraries Act ; and, benefiting by the experience of those towns which have preceded them, to do
better than them all. There have yet also to arise many wise
and generous men who will choose for their life-work and
their monument the formation and endowment of Libraries
and Reading-rooms—mental and moral hospitals for the
nation, and the best means of placing the highest and noblest
works of human genius within the reach of the humble and
the poor, and of raising and refining our national life.

FREE LIBRARIES AND NEWSROOMS FOR LONDON.

It is a serious discredit to the management of the metro-
polis that with all its wealth, intelligence, and energy, it
is so short of Free Libraries for the People ; great Reading
Rooms, where its clerks, artisans, etc., might spend their
evenings in quiet, pleasant and improving study ; and great
Lending Libraries, from whence the literature of England,
and indeed of the world, can be freely and safely distributed
to the homes of the people. It may be supposed that what
is found so advantageous in the provinces, would do as much,
if not more good in London.

The British Museum Library is certainly not suitable for
popular use, it is and should be rather a Museum of Books
than a Library for common use. It is not so much a lounge
to sit and read in for pleasure as the final resource for what

* Glasgow has been splendidly helped to a decision by a gift of some
seventy thousand pounds, wherewith to form and endow a Free Library,
and Leeds now has the most extensive Free Library system in the kingdom.

cannot be got elsewhere; that it meets this want for the nation is sufficient, neither in position or character is it fit to fill the place taken by popular Free Libraries and Newsrooms.

To those who know London it is not very hard to understand the causes which have worked against and which still hinder the adoption of the Free Libraries Acts in the metropolitan parishes. It is not so much that London vestrymen are inferior in intelligence, judgment, and public spirit to the town councillors of the provinces, or that the residents of these parishes would not be glad to use the Libraries and Newsrooms; it is rather that the terror of more rates is for certain reasons more overpowering to the Londoner than to the men of the provinces.

In the provinces the rents of dwelling-houses are so moderate that men earning from twenty to sixty shillings per week almost invariably occupy the whole of a house, and only pay for it a rent of from ten to twenty pounds a year, made easy by being taken in weekly instalments. The Library rate is a penny in the pound per annum on the rent—or from ten to twenty pence in the year, and this again being collected with other rates in two instalments, the payment itself is so small and the mode of payment so easy, and the benefit—*i.e.*, a Newsroom for the ratepayer and Books for his family—so great, that no impost is more popular than the Library rate ; and if the Act of Parliament permitted it, many of the provincial towns would gladly raise the rate to twopence in the pound, instead of the penny now granted.

In London a very large number of clerks, artisans, small shopkeepers, etc. so far from living in houses of small rental, undertake the heavy charge or care of houses of a value of from forty to seventy, or eighty pounds per annum, and by letting these houses off in portions, manage, if they have good tenants, to live in some portion of the house themselves nearly if not quite rent free ; to these men, burdened with so heavy a rental and paying of course proportionate rates, the very mention of even a penny in the pound increase, is a sound of alarm. Again, speaking generally, men of about equal social position in London or Birmingham, will be found to pay vastly different rents and rates.

Hence the vigorous opposition in Islington, St. Pancras, and other places in London to the adoption of the Free Library Acts. But they have to be adopted in London yet. Great wealthy parishes like

Poplar,	with a rental of	£500,000	per annum,
Shoreditch,	„	£350,000	„
Marylebone,	„	£1,000,000	„
St. Pancras,	„	£1,000,000	„
Paddington,	„	£750,000	„
Strand,	„	£450,000	„
Westminster,	„	£550,000	„
Hackney,	„	£500,000	„
Islington,	„	£850,000	„
Whitechapel,	„	£300,000	„
Kensington,	„	£749,000	„
St. George's	„	£800,000	„
Chelsea,	„	£300,000	„

may well begin with a halfpenny or even a farthing rate, and have one Library and Newsroom just to show their use.

The statement that Londoners are more highly assessed for local rates than are the men of the provinces, is disproved by the Parliamentary Report on Local Taxation, which gives the assessment of Marylebone as 3s 4d and of Birmingham as 4s 6d in the pound.

If Londoners could only see a good Free Library and Newsroom in use in one of their parishes, they would not be long without one in every parish. Could the owner of Columbia Market or some such place be induced to give part of a building for the purpose, and a strong Committee be formed, with funds to open and sustain for a year or two a model Newsroom and Free Library, bright, spacious, handsome, well furnished, with abundance of illustrated and popular papers, and a good supply of inexpensive but useful Books, the demand for similar Institutions in other parts would soon be too strong to be resisted, and either by subscription or by rates, or by the two

2*

combined, London would have a score of Free Libraries and Newsrooms, instead of, I think, one, or at most, two.

FREE LIBRARIES FOR SMALL TOWNS, VILLAGES, ETC.

By the provisions of the Free Libraries Act of 1866, it is possible for small towns or villages, whose resources would not enable them to organize and sustain a Free Library for themselves, to join by arrangement, and payment of some small sum, the nearest town possessing a Free Library, and have Books from the same, either by sending for them to the central depôt, or by having cases of books sent at certain times to some person appointed to receive and issue them at the place where they are required.

When the great Central Free Library in Birmingham was first opened, so great was the hunger for books, not only in the town but in the surrounding district, that on market day it was found that men and women from the "black country" for many miles round, viz., West Bromwich, Bilston, Wednesbury, Willenhall, Dudley, Tipton, and even Wolverhampton, were not only using the Reference Library and Newsroom which are open to all comers, but were borrowing books to take home for the week: this was a privilege it was intended to reserve for residents in the town; it seemed hardly fair that Birmingham ratepayers should provide home reading for the surrounding district, and yet it was hard to refuse.

While, however, the difficulty was being considered, it remedied itself. Experiencing the pleasure of a Free Library in the neighbouring town, the users determined to have one at home; now all these little towns have Free Libraries and Newsrooms of their own. Something is certainly due to the big town for its example, but more to the pluck and energy of the small towns that followed the lead so well; no town is so surrounded by such a family of admirable Free Libraries.

Where this cannot be done, the next best thing is for the small places to avail themselves of the provision referred to above, and affiliate themselves to the nearest large Free Library.

An admirable Paper, read by Sir Redmond Barry at the first Conference of Librarians, describes how the great Library at Melbourne, Australia, sends out of its wealth of knowledge and pleasure to the small places in its neighbourhood; and there seems no reason why the Free Libraries in the principal towns of England should not send out their weekly or monthly chests of books to the small towns and villages, there to be issued and looked after by the schoolmaster or some such responsible person—the school-house being used at night, too, as a reading-room—and the whole carried on at a very small cost, such as might be met by a small vote from the rates.

APPENDIX I.

PUBLIC LIBRARIES ACT (IRELAND), 1855.

18 AND 19 VICTORIA, CAP. XL.

The earlier Acts having been repealed are not reprinted here.

An Act for further promoting the Establishment of Free Public
Libraries and Museums in *Ireland.*   [26*th June*, 1855.}

'WHEREAS it is expedient to amend the Act of the Sixteenth
and Seventeenth Years of Her present Majesty, Chapter One
hundred and one, and to give greater facilities for the Establishment in *Ireland* of free Public Libraries and Museums or
Schools of Science and Art;' Be it therefore enacted by the
Queen's most Excellent Majesty, by and with the Advice and
Consent of the Lords Spiritual and Temporal, and Commons, in
this present Parliament assembled, and by the Authority of the
same, as follows :

16 and 17
Vict. c. 101,
and Sec. 99
of 17 and 18
Vict. c. 103,
repealed.

I. The said Act of the Sixteenth and Seventeenth Years of
Her present Majesty, Chapter One hundred and one, and Section
Ninety-nine of the Towns Improvement Act (*Ireland*), 1854, are
hereby repealed : but such Repeal shall not invalidate or affect
anything already done in pursuance of either of such Acts ;
and all Public Libraries and Museums established in *Ireland*
under either of those Acts shall be considered as having been
established under this Act.

Short Title.

II. In citing this Act for any purpose whatever it shall be
sufficient to use the expression "The Public Libraries Act
(*Ireland*), 1855."

Interpreta-
tion of
Terms.

III. In the Construction and for the Purposes of this Act (if
not inconsistent with the Context or Subject Matter) the following Terms shall have the respective Meanings hereinafter
assigned to them ; that is to say " Town " shall mean and include any City, Borough, Town, or Place in which Commissioners, Trustees, or other Persons have been or shall be elected
or appointed under the Act of the Ninth Year of King *George*
the Fourth, Chapter Eighty-two, or the Towns Improvement Act (*Ireland*), 1854," or any Local or other Act or Acts
for paving, flagging, lighting, watching, cleansing, or otherwise
improving any City, Borough, Town, or Place, for the Execution of any such Act or Acts, or superintending the Execution

thereof, and in which there shall not be a Town Council or other such Body elected under the Act of the Third and Fourth Year of Her present Majesty, Chapter One hundred and eight or any other Charter granted in pursuance of such Act or any Act passed for the Amendment thereof; " Town Commissioners" shall mean the Commissioners, Trustees, or other Persons for the Time being elected or appointed under any such first-mentioned Acts as aforesaid ; " Town Fund " shall mean the Town Fund, or the Rates of Property vested in and under the Control and Direction of any Town Commissioners, and applicable to the Purposes of any such Acts ; " Town Rate " shall mean the Rate or Rates authorized to be levied by any such Town Commissioners ; " Mayor" shall include Lord Mayor ; " Clerk" shall mean, as regards an incorporated Borough, the Town Clerk of such Borough, and as regards a Town in which there shall be Town Commissioners, the Clerk appointed by the Town Commissioners ; " Householder" shall mean a Male Occupier of a Dwelling House, or of any Lands, Tenements, or Hereditaments within any Town or incorporated Borough, and entitled for the Time being to vote at Elections of Commissioners, Aldermen, or Councillors in any such Town or Borough.

IV. The Council or Board of Municipal Commissioners of any incorporated Borough in *Ireland* regulated under the said Act of the Third and Fourth Years of Her present Majesty, Chapter One hundred and eight, or any Charter granted in pursuance of such Act, or any Act passed for the Amendment thereof, the Population of which according to the then last Census thereof shall exceed Five thousand Persons, or the Town Commissioners of any Town in *Ireland* having such a Population as aforesaid, may, if they think fit, appoint a Time for a Public Meeting of the Householders of the Borough or Town, as the case may be, in order to determine whether this Act shall be adopted for the Borough or Town, and Ten Days Notice at least of the Time, Place, and Object of the Meeting shall be given by affixing the same on or near the Door of every Church and Chapel within the Borough or Town, and also by advertising the same in One or more of the Newspapers published or circulated within the Borough or Town Seven Days at least before the Day appointed for the Meeting, and if at such Meeting Two-thirds of such Persons as aforesaid then present shall determine that this Act ought to be adopted for the Borough or Town, the same shall thenceforth take effect and come into operation in such Borough or Town, as the case may

Act may be adopted in any Incorporated Borough or any Town.

be, and shall be carried into execution, in accordance with the Laws for the Time being in force relating to the Municipal Corporation of such Borough, or relating to such Town.

Expenses of carrying Act into execution to be paid out of the Fund of the Borough or Town.

V. The Expenses incurred in calling and holding the Meeting, whether this Act shall be adopted or not, and the Expenses of carrying this Act into execution in such Borough, shall be paid out of the Borough Fund, and in such Town out of the Town Fund ; and the Council or Board of Municipal Commissioners, or Town Commissioners, may levy as part of the Borough Rate or Town Rate, as the case may be, or by a separate Rate to be assessed and recovered in like manner as the Borough Rate or Town Rate, all Monies from Time to Time necessary for defraying such Expenses ; and district Accounts shall be kept of the Receipts, Payments, and Liabilities of the Council with reference to the Execution of this Act.

Accounts to be audited, and sent to Lord Lieutenant, &c.; to be deposited and open to Inspection.

VI. Such Accounts shall be audited in the same way as all other Accounts of such Borough or Town respectively are audited, and the said Council or Board or Town Commissioners shall, within One Month after the same shall have been audited, transmit to the Lord Lieutenant or other Chief Governor or Governors of *Ireland* for the Time being a true and correct Copy of such Accounts ; and shall also within the Time aforesaid cause a Copy of such Accounts to be deposited in the Office of the Clerk ; and the said Accounts shall be open to the Inspection of all Householders of such Borough or Town respectively, and Copies thereof shall be delivered to any such Householder applying for the same, upon Payment of a reasonable Charge for the same, to be fixed by the Council or Board or Town Commissioners, as the case may be.

Incorporation of Commissioners of Towns for the Purposes of this Act.

VII. The Town Commissioners of every Town adopting this Act shall for the Purposes thereof be a Body Corporate, with perpetual Succession, by the Name of "The Commissioners for Public Libraries and Museums for the Town of
in the County of   ," and by that Name may sue and be sued, and hold and dispose of Lands, and use a Common Seal.

Rate not to exceed One Penny in the Pound, &c.

VIII. The Amount of the Rate to be levied in any Borough or Town in any One Year for the purposes of this Act shall not exceed the sum of One Penny in the Pound, and in any such Borough shall be assessed, raised, collected, and levied in the same manner as the Borough Rate, and in any such Town shall be assessed, raised, collected in the same manner as the Town Rate.

IX. The Council or Board of any Borough and the Town Commissioners of any Town respectively may from Time to Time, with the approval of Her Majesty's Treasury, appropriate for the purposes of this Act any Lands vested, as the case may be, in a Borough in the Mayor, Alderman, and Burgesses, and in a Town in the Town Commissioners, and may also, with such approval, purchase or rent any Lands or any suitable Buildings, and the Council or Board and Town Commissioners respectively may, upon any Lands so appropriated, purchased, or rented respectively, erect any Buildings suitable for Public Libraries or Museums or Schools of Science and Art, or both, and may apply, take down, alter, and extend any Buildings for such Purposes, and rebuild, repair, and improve the same respectively, and fit up, furnish, and supply the same respectively, with all requisite Furniture, Fittings, and Conveniences. *Lands, &c., may be appropriated, purchased, or rented for the Purposes of this Act.*

X. The Lands Clauses Consolidation Act, 1845, shall be incorporated with this Act; but the Council or Board, and Commissioners respectively shall not purchase or take any Lands otherwise than by Agreement. *Provisions of 8 and 9 Vict. c. 18, incorporated.*

XI. The Council or Board and Commissioners aforesaid respectively may, with the like approval as is required for the Purchase of Lands, sell any Lands vested in the Mayor, Aldermen, and Burgesses, or Board, or Town Commissioners respectively for the Purposes of this Act, or exchange the same for any Lands better adapted for the Purposes; and the Monies to arise from such Sale, or to be received for Equality of Exchange, or a sufficient Part thereof, shall be applied in or towards the Purchase of other Lands better adapted for such Purposes. *Lands, &c., may be sold or exchanged.*

XII. The general Management, Regulation, and Control of such Libraries and Museums or Schools of Science and Art shall be, as to any Borough, vested in and exercised by the Council or Board, and as to any Town, in and by the Town Commissioners, or such Committee as they respectively may from Time to Time appoint, who may from Time to Time purchase and provide the necessary Fuel, Lighting, and other similar matters, Books, Newspapers, Maps, and Specimens of Art and Science for the Use of the Library or Museum, and cause the same to be bound or repaired, when necessary, and appoint salaried Officers and Servants, and dimiss the same, and make Rules and Regulations for the Safety and Use of the Libraries and Museums or Schools of Science and Art, and for the Admission of Visitors. *General Management to be vested in Council or Board, or Town Commissioners.*

XIII. The Lands and Buildings so to be appropriated, pur- *In whom Property of*

Library, &c., to be vested. chased, or rented as aforesaid, and all other Real and Personal Property whatever presented to or purchased for any Library or Museum or School of Science and Art established under this Act, shall be vested, in the case of a Borough, in the Mayor, Aldermen, and Burgesses, and in the case of a Town in the Town Commissioners.

In case First Meeting decide not to adopt Act. XIV. If any Meeting called as herein-before provided to consider as to the Adoption of this Act for any Borough or Town shall determine against such adoption, no Meeting for a similar Purpose shall be held for the space of One Year at least from the Time of holding the previous Meeting.

Museums to be free. XV. The Admission to all Libraries and Museums established under this Act shall be open to the Public free of all charge.

This Act to be incorporated with Local Acts in force in Borough or Town. XVI. Upon the coming into operation of this Act in any Borough it shall as regards such Borough be incorporated with the said Act of the Third and Fourth *Victoria*, Chapter One hundred and eight, and upon the coming into operation of this Act in any Town, it shall, as regards such Town, be incorporated with the Act or Acts in force therein relating to the Powers and Duties of the Town Commissioners.

"PUBLIC LIBRARIES ACT, 1855," [ENGLAND].

18 & 19 VICTORIÆ, CAP. LXX.

An Act for further promoting the Establishment of Free Public Libraries and Museums in Municipal Towns, and for extending it to Towns governed under Local Improvement Acts, and to Parishes. [*30th July*, 1855.]

'WHEREAS it is expedient to amend and extend the Public Libraries Act, 1850:' Be it therefore enacted by the Queen's most Excellent Majesty, by and with the Advice and Consent of the Lords Spiritual and Temporal, and Commons, in this present Parliament assembled, and by the Authority of the same, as follows :

13 and 14 Vict. c. 65, repealed. I. The Public Libraries Act, 1850, is hereby repealed ; but such Repeal shall not invalidate or affect anything already done in pursuance of the same Act, and all Libraries and Museums established under that Act or the Act thereby repealed shall be considered as having been established under this Act, and the Council of any Borough which may have adopted the said Act of One thousand eight hundred and fifty, or established a Museum

under the Act thereby repealed, shall have and may use and
exercise all the Benefits, Privileges, and Powers given by this
Act; and all Monies which have been borrowed by virtue of the
said repealed Acts or either of them, and still remaining unpaid,
and the Interest thereof, shall be charged on the Borough Rates,
or a Rate to be assessed and recovered in the like manner as a
Borough Rate to be made by virtue of this Act.

II. In citing this Act for any Purposes whatever, it shall be Short Title
sufficient to use the Expression "The Public Libraries Act, of Act.
1855."

III. In the construction of this Act the following Words and Interpreta-
Expressions shall, unless there be something in the Subject or tion of
Context repugnant to such Construction, have the following Terms.
Meanings assigned to them respectively; that is to say "Parish"
shall mean every Place maintaining its own Poor; "Vestry"
shall mean the Inhabitants of the Parish lawfully assembled in
Vestry, or for any of the Purposes for which Vestries are holden,
except in those Parishes in which there is a Select Vestry elected
under the Act of the Fifty-ninth Year of King *George* the Third,
Chapter Twelve, or under the Act of the First and Second Years
of King *William* the Fourth, Chapter Sixty, or under the Provisions of any Local Act of Parliament for the Government of
any Parish by Vestries, in which Parishes it shall mean such
Select Vestry, and shall also mean any Body of Persons, by whatever Name distinguished, acting by virtue of any Act of Parliament, Prescription, Custom or otherwise, as or instead of a Vestry
or Select Vestry; "Ratepayers" shall mean all Persons for the
Time being assessed to Rates for the Relief of the Poor of the
Parish; "Overseers of the Poor" shall mean also any Persons
authorized and required to make and collect the Rate for the
Relief of the Poor of the Parish, and acting instead of Overseers
of the Poor; "Board" shall mean the Commissioners, Trustees,
or other Body of Persons, by whatever Name distinguished, for the
Time being in Office and acting in the execution of any Improve-
ment Act, being an Act for draining, cleansing, paving, lighting,
watching, or otherwise improving a Place, or for any of those
Purposes; "Improvement Rates" shall mean the Rates, Tolls,
Rents, Income, and other Monies whatsoever which, under the
Provisions of any such Improvement Act, shall be applicable
for the general purposes of such Act.

IV. The Mayor of any Municipal Borough the Population of Town Coun-
which, according to the then last Census thereof, shall exceed cils of certain.
Five Thousand Persons, shall, on the Request of the Town Boroughs
may adopt

determined
by Inhabi-
tants.

Council, convene a Public Meeting of the Burgesses of the
Borough, in order to determine whether this Act shall be adopted
for the Municipal Borough, and Ten Days Notice at least of the
Time, Place, and Object of the Meeting shall be given by affixing
the same on or near the Door of every Church and Chapel within
the Borough, and also by advertising the same in One or more of
the Newspapers published or circulated within the Borough,
Seven Days at least before the Day appointed for the Meeting ;
and if at such Meeting Two-thirds of such Persons as aforesaid
then present shall determine that this Act ought to be adopted
for the Borough, the same shall thenceforth take effect and come
into operation in such Borough, and shall be carried into execution in accordance with the Laws for the Time being in force
relating to the Municipal Corporation of such Borough : Provided always, that the Mayor, or, in his absence, the Chairman
of the Meeting, shall cause a Minute to be made of the Resolutions of the Meeting, and shall sign the same ; and the Resolutions so signed shall be conclusive Evidence that the Meeting
was duly convened, and the Vote thereat duly taken, and that
the Minute contains a true Account of the Proceedings thereat.

Expenses of
carrying
Act into exe-
cution in a
Borough to
be paid out of
the Borough
Fund.

V. The Expenses incurred in calling and holding the Meeting, whether this Act shall be adopted or not, and the Expenses
of carrying this Act into execution in such Borough, may be
paid out of the Borough Fund, and the Council may levy by a
separate Rate, to be called a Library Rate, to be made and
recoverable in the manner hereinafter provided, all Monies from
Time to Time necessary for defraying such Expenses ; and distinct Accounts shall be kept of the Receipts, Payments, and
Liabilities of the Council with reference to the Execution of this
Act.

Board of any
District
withinLimits
of any Im-
provement
Act may
adopt this
Act if deter-
mined by In-
habitants.

VI. The Board of any District, being a Place within the Limits
of any Improvement Act, and having such a Population as aforesaid, shall, upon the Requisition in Writing of at least Ten
Persons assessed to and paying the Improvement Rate, appoint a
Time not less than Ten Days nor more than Twenty Days from
the Time of receiving such Requisition for a Public Meeting of
the Persons assessed to and paying such Rate in order to determine whether this Act shall be adopted for such District, and
Ten Days Notice at least of the Time, Place, and Object of such
Meeting shall be given, by affixing the same on or near the Door
of every Church and Chapel within the District, and also by
advertising the same in One or more of the Newspapers published
or circulated within the District, Seven Days at least before the

Day appointed for the Meeting; and if at such Meeting Two-thirds of such Persons as aforesaid then present shall determine that this Act ought to be adopted for the District, the same shall henceforth take effect, and come into operation in such District, and shall be carried into effect according to the Laws for the Time being in force relating to such Board.

VII. The Expenses incurred in calling and holding the Meeting whether this Act shall be adopted or not, and the Expenses of carrying this Act into execution in any such District, shall be paid out of the Improvement Rate, and the Board may levy as Part of the Improvement Rate, or by a separate Rate to be assessed and recovered in like manner as an Improvement Rate, such Sums of Money as shall be from Time to Time necessary for defraying such Expenses; and the Board shall keep distinct Accounts of their Receipts, Payments, Credits and Liabilities with reference to the Execution of this Act, which Accounts shall be audited in the same Way as Accounts are directed to be audited under the Improvement Act. *Expenses of carrying Act into execution to be charged on Improvement Rate.*

VIII. Upon the Requisition in Writing of at least Ten Rate-payers of any Parish having such a Population as aforesaid, the Overseers of the Poor shall appoint a Time, not less than Ten Days nor more than Twenty Days from the Time of receiving such requisition, for a Public Meeting of the Ratepayers in order to determine whether this Act shall be adopted for the Parish; and Ten Days Notice at least of the Time, Place, and Object of the Meeting shall be given by affixing the same on or near the Door of every Church and Chapel within the Parish, and also by advertising the same in One or more of the Newspapers published or circulated within the Parish, Seven Days at least before the Day appointed for the Meeting; and if at such Meeting Two-thirds of the Ratepayers then present shall determine that this Act ought to be adopted for such Parish, the same shall come into operation in such Parish, and the Vestry shall forthwith appoint not less than Three nor more than Nine Rate-payers Commissioners for carrying the Act into execution, who shall be a Body Corporate by the Name of " The Commissioners for Public Libraries and Museums for the Parish of   in the County of   ," and by that name may sue and be sued, and hold and dispose of Lands, and use a Common Seal: Provided always, that in any Parish where there shall not be a greater Population than Eight thousand Inhabitants by the then last Census, it shall be lawful for any Ten Ratepayers to deliver a Requisition by them signed, and describing their *Certain Parishes may adopt this Act with the Consent of Two-thirds of the Rate-payers.*   *The Vestry to appoint Commissioners for carrying the Act into execution who shall be a Body Corporate.*

Place of Residence, to the Overseers or One of the Overseers of the said Parish, requiring the Votes of the Ratepayers at such Meeting to be taken according to the Provisions of the Act passed in the Fifty-eighth Year of the Reign of King *George* the Third, Chapter Sixty-nine, and the Votes at such Meeting shall thereupon be taken according to the Provisions of the said last-mentioned Act of Parliament, and not otherwise.

One-third of such Commissioners to go out of Office yearly and others to be appointed, &c.

IX. At the Termination of every Year (the Year being reckoned from and exclusive of the Day of the First Appointment of Commissioners) a Meeting of the Vestry shall be held, at which Meeting One-third, or as nearly as may be One-third of the Commissioners, to be determined by Ballot, shall go out of Office, and the Vestry shall appoint other Commissioners in their Place, but the outgoing Commissioners may be re-elected; and the Vestry shall fill up every Vacancy among the Commissioners, whether occurring by Death, Resignation, or otherwise, as soon as possible after the same occurs.

General and Special Meetings of Commissioners.

X. The Commissioners shall meet at least once in every Calendar Month, and at such other Times as they think fit, at the Public Library or Museum or some other convenient Place; and any one Commissioner may summon a Special Meeting of the Commissioners by giving Three clear Days Notice in Writing to each Commissioner, specifying therein the Purpose for which the Meeting is called; and no Business shall be transacted at any Meeting of the Commissioners unless at least Two Commissioners shall be present.

Minutes of Proceedings of Commissioners to be entered in Books.

XI. All Orders and Proceedings of the Commissioners shall be entered in Books to be kept by them for that Purpose, and shall be signed by the Commissioners or any Two of them; and all such Orders and Proceedings so entered and purporting to be so signed shall be deemed to be original Orders and Proceedings, and such Books may be produced and read as Evidence of all such Orders and Proceedings upon any judicial Proceeding whatsoever.

Distinct Accounts to be kept by Commissioners, and duly audited.

XII. The Commissioners shall keep distinct and regular Accounts of their Receipts, Payments, Credits, and Liabilities with reference to the Execution of this Act, which Accounts shall be audited yearly by the Poor-Law Auditor, if the Accounts of the Poor-Rate Expenditure of the Parish be audited by a Poor-Law Auditor, but if not so audited then by Two Auditors not being Commissioners, who shall be yearly appointed by the Vestry, and the Auditor or Auditors shall report thereon, but such Report shall be laid before the Vestry by the Commissioners.

XIII. The Expenses of calling and holding the Meeting of the Ratepayers, whether this Act shall be adopted or not, and the Expenses of carrying this Act into execution in any Parish, to such Amount as shall be from Time to Time sanctioned by the Vestry, shall be paid out of a Rate to be made and recovered in like Manner as a Poor Rate, except that every Person occupying Lands used as Arable, Meadow, or Pasture Ground only, or as Woodlands, or Market Gardens or Nursery Grounds, shall be rated in respect of the same in the Proportion of One-third Part only of the full net annual Value thereof respectively; the Vestry to be called for the Purpose of sanctioning the Amount shall be convened in the Manner usual in the Parish; the Amount for the Time being proposed to be raised for such Expenses shall be expressed in the Notice convening the Vestry, and shall be paid, according to the Order of the Vestry, to such Person as shall be appointed by the Commissioners to receive the same: Provided always, that in the Notices requiring the Payment of the Rate there shall be stated the Proportion which the Amount to be thereby raised for the Purposes of this Act shall bear to the total Amount of the Rate.

Expenses of executing Act in any Parish to be paid out of Poor Rate.

XIV. The Vestries of any Two or more neighbouring Parishes having according to the then last Census an aggregate Population exceeding Five Thousand Persons may adopt this Act, in like manner as if the Population of each of those Parishes according to the then last Census exceeded Five Thousand, and may concur in carrying the same into execution in such Parishes for such Time as they shall mutually agree: and such Vestries may decide that a Public Library or Museum, or both, shall be erected in any One of such Parishes, and that the Expenses of carrying this Act into execution with reference to the same shall be borne by such Parishes in such Proportions as such Vestries shall mutually approve; the Proportion for each of such Parishes of such Expenses shall be paid out of the Monies to be raised for the Relief of the Poor of the same respective Parishes accordingly; but no more than Three Commissioners shall be appointed for each Parish; and the Commissioners so appointed for each of such Parishes shall in the Management of the said Public Library and Museum form One Body of Commissioners, and shall act accordingly in the execution of this Act; and the Accounts of the Commissioners shall be examined and reported on by the Auditor or Auditors of such Parishes; and the surplus Money at the Disposal as aforesaid of such Commissioners shall be paid to the Overseers of such Parishes respectively, in the

Vestries of Two or more neighbouring Parishes may adopt the Act.

Proportion in which such Parishes shall be liable to such Expenses.

Rates levied not to exceed One Penny in the Pound.

XV. The Amount of the Rate to be levied in any Borough, District, or Parish in any One Year for the Purposes of this Act shall not exceed the Sum of One Penny in the Pound ; and for the Purposes of the Library Rate all the Clauses of the Towns Improvement Clauses Act, 1847, with respect to the Manner of making Rates, to the Appeal to be made against any Rate, and to the Recovery of Rates, shall be incorporated with this Act ; and whenever the Words " Special Act" occur in the Act so incorporated they shall mean " The Public Libraries Act, 1855 ;"

Accounts of Board and Commissioners to be open to Inspection.

the Accounts of the said Board and Commissioners respectively with reference to the Execution of this Act shall at all reasonable Times be open, without Charge, to the Inspection of every Person rated to the Improvement Rate or to the Rates for the Relief of the Poor of the Parish, as the Case may be, who may make Copies of or Extracts from such Accounts, without paying for the same ; and in case the Board or the Commissioners, or any of them respectively, or any of their respective Officers or Servants having the Custody of such Accounts, shall not permit the same Accounts to be inspected, or Copies of or Extracts from the same to be made, every Person so offending shall for every such offence forfeit any Sum not exceeding Five Pounds.

Power to Council, &c., to borrow on Mortgage.

XVI. For carrying this Act into execution the Council, Board, or Commissioners respectively may, with the Approval of Her Majesty's Treasury, (and as to the Commissioners, with the Sanction also of the Vestry and the Poor Law Board,) from Time to Time borrow at Interest on the Security of a Mortgage or Bond of the Borough Fund, or of the Rates levied in pursuance of this Act, such Sums of Money as may be by them respectively required ; and the Commissioners for carrying into execution the Act of the Ninth and Tenth Years of Her Majesty, Chapter Eighty, may from Time to Time advance and lend any such sums of Money.

Provisions of 8 and 9 Vict. c. 16, as to Borrowing, extended to this Act.

XVII. The Clauses and Provisions of "The Companies Clauses Consolidation Act, 1845," with respect to the borrowing of Money on Mortgage or Bond, and the Accountability of Officers, and the Recovery of Damages and Penalties, so far as such Provisions may respectively be applicable to the Purposes of this Act, shall be respectively incorporated with this Act.

Lands, &c., may be appropriated, purchased or

XVIII. The Council of any Borough and the Board of any District respectively may from Time to Time, with the Approval of Her Majesty's Treasury, appropriate for the Purposes of this Act any Lands vested, as the Case may be, in a Borough, in the Mayor, Aldermen, and Burgesses, and in a District in the Board, and the Council, Board, and Commissioners respectively may also, with such Approval, purchase or rent any Lands or any suitable Buildings ; and the Council and Board and Commissioners respectively may, upon any Lands so appropriated, purchased, or rented respectively, erect any Buildings suitable for Public Libraries or Museums, or both, or for Schools for Science or Art, and may apply, take down, alter, and extend any Buildings for such Purposes, and rebuild, repair, and improve the same respectively, and fit up, furnish, and supply the same respectively with all requisite Furniture, Fittings, and Conveniences. *rented for the Purposes of this Act.*

XIX. " The Lands Clauses Consolidation Act, 1845," shall be incorporated with this Act; but the Council Board, and Commissioners respectively shall not purchase or take any Lands otherwise than by Agreement. *8 and 9 Vict. c. 18, incorporated.*

XX. The Council, Board, and Commissioners aforesaid respectively may, with the like Approval as is required for the Purchase of Lands, sell any Lands vested in the Mayor, Aldermen, and Burgesses, or Board or Commissioners respectively, for the Purposes of this Act, or exchange the same for any Lands better adapted for the Purposes ; and the Monies to arise from such Sale or to be received for Equality of Exchange, or a sufficient part thereof, shall be applied in or towards the Purchase of other Lands better adapted for such Purposes. *Lands, &c. may be sold or exchanged.*

XXI. The general Management, Regulation and Control of such Libraries and Museums, Schools for Science and Art, shall be, as to any Borough, vested in and exercised by the Council, and as to any District in and by the Board, and as to any Parish or Parishes in and by the Commissioners, or such Committee as such Council or Board may from Time to Time appoint, the Members whereof need not be Members of the Council or Board or be Commissioners, who may from Time to Time purchase and provide the necessary Fuel, Lighting, and other similar Matters, Books, Newspapers, Maps, and Specimens of Art and Science, for the Use of the Library or Museum, or School, and cause the same to be bound or repaired when necessary, and appoint salaried Officers and Servants, and dismiss the same, and make Rules and Regulations for the Safety and Use of the Libraries and Museums, and Schools, and for the Admission of the Public. *General Management to be vested in Council, Board, or Commissioners.*

XXII. The Lands and Buildings so to be appropriated, pur- *Property of*

Library, &c., chased, or rented as aforesaid, and all other Real and Personal
to be vested
in Council, Property whatever presented to or purchased for any Library or
&c.   Museum established under this Act, or School, shall be vested, in
the Case of a Borough, in the Mayor, Aldermen, and Burgesses,
in the Case of a District in the Board, and in the Case of a
Parish or Parishes in the Commissioners.

If Meeting   XXIII. If any Meeting called as aforesaid to determine as to
does not
adopt Act,   the Adoption of this Act for any Borough, District, or Parish
no other   shall determine against the Adoption, no Meeting for a similar
Meeting to
be held for a Purpose shall be held for the Space of One Year at least from
Year.   the time of holding the previous Meeting.

Act may be   XXIV. The Lord Mayor of the City of *London* shall, on the
adopted in
the City of   Request of the Lord Mayor, Aldermen, and Commons of the
London if   City of *London*, in Common Council assembled, convene a Public
Two-thirds
of Persons   Meeting in manner herein-before mentioned of all Persons rated
rated to the and assessed to the Consolidated Rate in the City of *London*, in
Consolidated
Rate,   order to determine whether this Act should be adopted in the
assembled at
a Public   said City; and if at such Meeting Two-thirds of such Persons
Meeting,   then present shall determine that this Act ought to be adopted
assent.
for the City of *London*, the same shall henceforth take effect
and come into operation in the City of *London*, and shall be carried into execution in accordance with the Laws for the Time
being in force relating to the City of *London* : Provided always,
that the Resolution of such Public Meeting, signed by the Lord
Mayor, shall be reported to the said Lord Mayor, Aldermen, and
Commons, in Common Council assembled, and entered on the
Minutes thereof, and that such Entry shall be Evidence; the
Expenses incurred in calling and holding the Meeting, whether
this Act shall be adopted or not, and the Expenses of carrying
this Act into execution in the City of *London*, shall be paid out
of the Consolidated Rate, and the Commissioners of Sewers of
the City of London may levy a part of the Consolidated Rate,
or, by a separate Rate, to be assessed and recovered in like
Manner as the Consolidated Rate, all Monies from Time to
Time necessary for defraying such Expenses, and distinct Accounts shall be kept of the Receipts, Payments, and Liabilities
of the said Lord Mayor, Aldermen, and Commons with reference
to the Execution of the Act.

Museums to   XXV. The Admission to all Libraries and Museums estab-
be free.
lished under this Act shall be open to the Public free of all
Charge.

Extent of   XXVI. This Act shall not extend to *Ireland* or *Scotland*.
Act.

PUBLIC LIBRARIES AMENDMENT ACT (ENGLAND AND SCOTLAND), 1866.

29 AND 30 VICTORIÆ, CAP. CXIV.

An Act to amend the "Public Libraries Act." [10th August, 1866.]

'WHEREAS it is expedient to amend "The Public Libraries Act, 1855," and to assimilate the Laws relating to Public Libraries in *England* and *Scotland :*' Be it therefore enacted by the Queen's most excellent Majesty, by and with the Advice and Consent of the Lords Spiritual and Temporal, and Commons, in this present Parliament assembled, and by the Authority of the same as follows : *(margin: 18 and 19 Vict. c. 95.)*

1. So much of the Section Fifteen of the said "Public Libraries Act, 1855," as incorporates with that Act certain Clauses of "The Towns Improvement Clauses Act, 1847," shall, so far as the same relates to or concerns Municipal Boroughs, be repealed. *(margin: Towns Improvement Clauses Act not to apply to Boroughs.)*

2. Section Five of the said Act, except so much thereof as relates to keeping distinct Accounts, shall be repealed; and the Expenses incurred in calling and holding the Meeting, whether the said Act shall be adopted or not, and the Expenses of carrying the said Act into execution in any Municipal Borough, may be paid out of the Borough Rate of such Borough, or by and out of a Rate to be made and recovered in such Borough, in like manner as a Borough Rate may be made and recovered therein, but the Amount so paid in such Borough in any One Year shall not exceed the sum of One Penny in the Pound upon the annual Value of the Property in such Borough rateable to a Borough Rate : Provided always, that nothing in this Act shall interfere with the Operation of the Act Twenty-eighth and Twenty-ninth *Victoria,* Chapter One hundred and eight, so far as it relates to the Collection of a Rate for a Public Library in the City of *Oxford.* *(margin: Part of Sec. 5 of recited Act repealed. Expenses of executing Act in Boroughs to be paid out of Borough Fund.)*

3. The Public Meeting mentioned in Section Four of the said "Public Libraries Act, 1855," shall be called either on the Request of the Town Council, or on the Request in Writing of Ten Ratepayers residing in the Borough. *(margin: Calling of Meeting in Boroughs.)*

4. Any Parish, of whatever Population, adjoining any Borough, District, or Parish which shall have adopted or shall contemplate the Adoption of the said "Public Libraries Act, 1855," may, with the Consent of more than One-half of the *(margin: Parishes adjoining a Borough, &c., may unite in adopting Act.)*

Ratepayers thereof present at a Meeting to be convened in manner
directed by the said Act with reference to Meetings of Ratepayers, and with the Consent also of the Town Council of such
Borough, or the Board of such District, or the Commissioners of
such Parish, as the Case may be, determine that such adjoining
Parish shall for the Purposes of the said Act form Part of such
Borough, District, or Parish, and thereupon the Vestry of such
adjoining Parish shall forthwith appoint Three Ratepayers
Commissioners for such Parish, One-third of whom shall go
out of Office, and the Vacancies be filled up as provided by the
said Act with respect to the Commissioners of a Parish, and such
Commissioners for the Time being shall for the Purposes of the
said Act be considered as Part of such Town Council, Board or
Commissioners as the Case may be; and the Expenses of calling
the Meeting, and the Proportion of the Expenses of such adjoining Parish of carrying the said Act into execution, shall be paid
out of the Poor Rates thereof to such Person as the Commissioners of the said adjoining Parish shall appoint to receive the
same.

Majority for Adoption of Act. 5. The Majority necessary to be obtained for the Adoption of
the said Act or "The Public Libraries Act (*Scotland*), 1854,"
shall be more than One-half of the Persons present at the Meeting, instead of Two-thirds of such Persons as now required.

Act applicable whatever Population may be. 6. "The Public Libraries Act (1855)" and "The Public
Libraries Act (*Scotland*) (1854)" shall be applicable to any
Borough, District, or Parish or Burgh, of whatever Population.

17 and 18 Vict. c. 64 ss. 6, 7, 8, repealed. 7. So much of Section Six of "The Public Libraries Act
(*Scotland*), 1854," as authorizes the demanding of a Poll, and
Sections Seven and Eight of the said Act, are hereby repealed.

If Burgh declines Act, no further Meeting for a Year. 8. If any Meeting called as provided by the said last-mentioned
Act shall determine against the Adoption of the Act in any
Burgh, no Meeting for a similar Purpose shall be held for the
Space of One Year at least from the Time of holding the
previous Meeting.

Parts of 8 and 9 Vict. cap. 17 extended 17 and 18th Vict. c. 64. 9. The Clauses and Provisions of "The Companies Clauses
Consolidation (*Scotland*) Act (1845)" with respect to the
borrowing of Money upon Mortgage or Bond, and the Accountability of Officers, and the Recovery of Damages and Penalties,
so far as such Provisions may respectively be applicable to the
Purposes of the said "Public Libraries Act (*Scotland*) (1854),"
shall be respectively incorporated with that Act.

A Library, &c., may be established 10. Wherever a Public Museum or Library has been established
under any Act relating to Public Libraries or Museums, or shall

hereafter be established under either of the said before-mentioned any Time be established in connexion therewith without any further Proceedings being taken under the said Acts. *in connexion with any Museum, &c.*

Acts, a Public Library or Museum, as the Case may be, may at

11. This Act may be cited as " The Public Libraries Amend- *Short Title.* ment Act (*England* and *Scotland*), 1866," and shall be taken to be Part of the said " Public Libraries Act, 1855," and shall be construed accordingly.

PUBLIC LIBRARIES ACT (SCOTLAND), 1867,

30 AND 31 VICTORIÆ, CAP. XXXVII.

An Act to amend and consolidate the Public Libraries Acts, (Scotland). [*15th July*, 1867.]

' WHEREAS it is expedient to amend and consolidate the Public Libraries Acts relating to *Scotland*, and to give greater facilities for the Formation and Establishment there of Public Libraries, Art Galleries, and Museums :'

Be it therefore enacted by the Queen's most Excellent Majesty, by and with the Advice and Consent of the Lords Spiritual and Temporal, and Commons, in this present Parliament assembled, and by the Authority of the same, as follows :—

I. The Public Libraries Act (*Scotland*), 1854, and so much of the Public Libraries Amendment Act (*England and Scotland*), 1866, as relates to *Scotland*, are hereby repealed, but such Repeal shall not invalidate or affect anything already done in pursuance of these Acts or either of them, and all Public Libraries and Museums established in *Scotland* under these Acts or either of them shall be held as coming under the operation of this Act. *17 and 18 Vict. c. 64, and so much of 29 and 30 Vict. c. 114, as relates to Scotland, repealed.*

II. In the Construction of this Act the following Words and Expressions shall have the Meanings hereby assigned, if not inconsistent with the Context or Subject Matter ; that is to say, *Interpretation of Terms.*

The Expression " Burgh " shall mean a Royal Burgh or a Burgh or Town to which Magistrates and Councils were provided by the Act of the Third and Fourth Years of King *William* the Fourth, Chapter Seventy-seven.

The Word " District " shall mean a Burgh of Barony, a Burgh of Regality, or any other populous Place, not being a Royal Burgh or a Town or Burgh to which Magistrates and Councils were provided by the said Act of the Third and Fourth

Years of King *William* the Fourth, Chapter Seventy-seven, where any Local or General Police Act is in force.

The Word "Board" in Parishes shall mean the Parochial Board acting under the Powers and in execution of the Act of the Eighth and Ninth *Victoria*, Chapter Eighty-three; and in Districts it shall mean the Commissioners, Trustees, or other Body of Persons, by whatever Name distinguished, for the Time being in Office and acting in execution of any Special, Local, or General Police Act.

The Word "Householders" in all Burghs shall mean all Persons entitled to vote in the Election of Members of Parliament, but in Districts it shall mean all Persons assessed under and for the Purposes of any Local or General Police Act which may be in force therein; and in Parishes it shall mean all Ratepayers under the Act of the Eighth and Ninth *Victoria*, Chapter Eighty-three.

The Expression "Police Rates" shall mean the Rates, Tolls, Rents, Income, and other Monies whatsoever which under the Provisions of any Police Act shall be applicable for the General Purposes of such Act.

Meeting to be called for considering the Adoption of this Act in any Burgh, District, or Parish.

III. Upon the Requisition in Writing of the Magistrates and Council or of Ten Householders in any Burgh, District, or Parish, the Chief or Senior Magistrate of such Burgh, or in the case of a District, or Parish, the Sheriff of the County or one of his Substitutes, shall, within Ten Days after the Receipt of such Requisition, convene a Meeting of Householders, and preside at the same for the Purpose of considering whether this Act shall be adopted for such Burgh, District or Parish, such Meeting to be held in any convenient Place on a Day not less than Twenty-one Days or more than Thirty Days after the Receipt of such Requisition; and Notice of the Time and Place of such Meeting shall be given by affixing the same upon the Doors of the Parish Churches within such Burgh, District, or Parish, and also by advertising the same in at least One Newspaper published or circulated within such Burgh, District or Parish, not less than Seven Days preceding the Day of Meeting.

Act may be adopted at Meeting by a Majority, &c.

IV. If at such Meeting it shall be determined by a Majority of Householders present that the Provisions of this Act shall be adopted in such Burgh, District, or Parish, then the same shall from thenceforth come into operation therein; and the Chairman and the Meeting shall cause a Minute to be made of the Resolutions of the Meeting, and shall sign the same.

Expenses of

V. The Expenses incurred in calling and holding such Meeting, whether this Act shall be adopted or not, and the Expenses carrying this Act into execution when adopted, shall, in the case of a Burgh or District, be paid out of the Police Rate, and the Magistrates and Council of such Burgh, or the Board of such District, shall yearly levy as part of the Police Rate, or by a separate Rate, to be made, levied, and recovered by the Magistrates and Council of such Burgh or the Board of such District in such and the like Manner, from the same Descriptions of Persons and Property, and with and under the like Powers, Provisions, and Exceptions as the General Assessments leviable under the Acts of the Thirteenth and Fourteenth *Victoria*, Chapter Thirty-three (in the Case of Burghs or Districts which on or before the First Day of *August*, One thousand eight hundred and sixty-two, had adopted in whole or in part the Act of the Thirteenth and Fourteenth *Victoria*, Chapter Thirty-three), and of the Twenty-fifth and Twenty-sixth *Victoria*, Chapter One hundred and one (in the Case of all other Burghs or Districts), for Police and other Purposes, are authorized to be made, levied, and recovered, and as if such Magistrates and Council or the Board of such District were Commissioners elected under any of these Acts respectively, and the said Assessments were Part of the General Assessments authorized to be thereby made ; and in the Case of a Parish the Board shall pay the Expenses aforesaid out of a Rate to be made, levied, and recovered in like Manner, and from the same Description of Persons and Property, and with and under the like Powers, Provisions, and Exceptions, as the Poor Rate leviable under the Act of the Eighth and Ninth *Victoria*, Chapter Eighty-three : Provided always, that nothing herein contained shall prevent the City of *Glasgow* or any other Place from levying a Rate for the Purposes of this Act, in conformity with the Provisions of any local Police Act which may for the Time being be in force in said City of *Glasgow* or other Place.

carrying this Act into execution in Burghs and Districts to be paid out of the Police Rates.

VI. The Amount of the Rate to be so levied for the Purposes of this Act in any Burgh, District, or Parish in any One Year shall not exceed the Sum of One Penny in the Pound of yearly Rent, and the Magistrates and Council of any Burgh, or the Board of any District or Parish, shall provide and keep Books in which shall be entered true and regular Accounts of their Receipts, Payments, and Liabilities with reference to the Execution of this Act, to be called " The Public Libraries Account ;" and such Books shall, without Fee or Reward, and at all reasonable Times, be open to the Inspection of every Person liable to

Rate levied not to exceed the Sum of One Penny in the Pound of Yearly Rent.

The Accounts of the Magistrates and Council, or the Board

be assessed by virtue of this Act, who respectively may, without paying for the same, take Copies of or make Extracts from such Books; and in case such Magistrates and Council of any Burgh, or Board of any District or Parish, or any of them respectively, or any of their respective Officers or Servants having the Custody of such Books, shall not permit the same to be inspected, or Copies or Extracts from the Accounts to be made or taken, every Person so offending shall for every such Offence forfeit any Sum not exceeding Five Pounds, such Penalty to be recovered before the Sheriff or Justices of the Peace in like Manner as provided for the Recovery of Small Debts, and to be applied when recovered towards the Purposes of this Act. .

of any District or Parish, to be open to Inspection.

VII. For carrying this Act into execution, the Magistrates and Council of any Burgh, or the Board of any District or Parish respectively may from Time to Time borrow at Interest on the Security of a Mortgage or Bond of the Rates to be levied in pursuance of this Act, such Sums of Money, to be repaid by yearly Instalments within a Period not exceeding Thirty Years, as may be by them respectively required; and the Commissioners for carrying into execution the Act of the Ninth and Tenth *Victoria,* Chapter Eighty, may, with the Consent of the Commissioners of her Majesty's Treasury, from Time to Time advance and lend such Sums of Money.

Power to Council or Board to borrow on Mortgage or Bond.

VIII. The Clauses and Provisions of " The Companies Clauses Consolidation (*Scotland*) Act, 1845," with respect to the borrowing of Money on Mortgage or Bond, and the Accountability of Officers, and the Recovery of Damages and Penalties, so far as such Provisions may respectively be applicable to the Purposes of this Act, shall be held as incorporated with this Act.

Provisions of 8 and 9 Vict. c. 17, as to Borrowing Powers, extended to this Act.

IX. The Boundaries of Burghs and Districts shall be the same as the Boundaries declared for such Burghs and Districts by and for the Purposes of the Acts of the Thirteenth and Fourteenth *Victoria,* Chapter Thirty-three, and Twenty-fifth and Twenty-sixth *Victoria,* Chapter One hundred and one, or any Local Police Act which may for the Time being be in force in any such Burghs or Districts.

Boundaries of Burghs, &c.

X. The Magistrates and Council of any Burgh or the Board of any District or Parish, as the Case may be, may from Time to Time appropriate for the Purposes of this Act any Lands or Buildings vested in them, and also out of the Rates levied or Money borrowed as herein provided, purchase, feu, or rent any Land or any suitable Building, and may upon any Land so appropriated, rented, feued, or purchased, erect any Buildings suit-

Lands, &c., may be appropriated, purchased, or rented for the Purposes of this Act.

able for Public Libraries, Art Galleries, or Museums, or each respectively, and may alter or extend any Buildings for such Purposes, and repair and improve the same respectively, and fit up, furnish, and supply the same respectively with all requisite Furniture, Fittings, and Conveniences.

XI. All the Clauses and Provisions of the "Lands Clauses Consolidation Act (*Scotland*), 1845," with respect to the Purchase of Lands by Agreement, and with respect to the Purchase Money or Compensation coming to Parties having limited Interests, or prevented from treating, or not making a Title, and also with respect to Conveyances of Lands, so far as the same Clauses and Provisions respectively are applicable to the Cases contemplated by the last Section, shall be held as incorporated in this Act; and the Expression "the Special Act," used in the said Clauses and Provisions, shall be construed to mean this Act; and the Expression "the Promoters of the Undertaking," used in the same Clauses and Provisions, shall be construed to mean 'the Magistrates and Council of the Burgh or the Board of the District or Parish in question. *Certain Clauses of 8 and 9 Vict. c. 19 incorporated with this Act.*

XII. The Magistrates and Council of any Burgh and the Board of any District or Parish may sell any Land, Buildings, or other Property better adapted for the Purposes, and may also sell or exchange any Books, Works of Art, or other Property of which there may be Duplicates; and the Monies to arise from such Sale or Exchange shall be applied for the Purposes of this Act. *Lands, &c., may be sold or exchanged.*

XIII. The Lands and Buildings so to be appropriated, purchased, or rented, and all other Real or Personal Property whatever presented to or purchased for any Library, Art Gallery, or Museum established under this Act, shall, in the Case of a Burgh, be vested in the Magistrates and Council, and in the Case of a District or Parish, in the Board. *Property of Library, &c., vested in Magistrates, &c.*

XIV. The Magistrates and Council of any Burgh or the Board of any District or Parish where this Act has been adopted, shall, within One Month after its Adoption, and thereafter from Year to Year, in the Case of a Burgh at the First Meeting after the annual Election of Town Councillors. in the Case of a District at the first Meeting after the annual Election of Police Commissioners, and in the Case of a Parish at the First Meeting after the annual Meeting for the Election of representative Members of the Parochial Board, appoint a Committee, consisting of not more than Twenty Members, Half of whom shall be Magistrates and Members of the Council or Members of the Board respec- *General Management to be vested in a Committee appointed by Magistrates and Councils of Burghs, and Boards of Districts or Parishes.*

tively, and the remaining Half shall be chosen by the Council or
Board from amongst the Householders not Members of the
Council or Board within such Burgh, District, or Parish, as the
Case may be, Three to be a Quorum ; and such Committee so
appointed shall have Power, under the Authority of the Magis-
trates and Council or Board, as the Case may be, to purchase
Books, Newspapers, Reviews, Magazines, and other Periodicals,
Statuary, Pictures, Engravings, Maps, and Specimens of Art and
Science, for the Establishment, Increase, and Use of such Libraries, Art Galleries and Museums, and to do all things necessary for keeping the same in a proper state of Preservation and
Repair; and such Committee, subject as aforesaid, shall manage,.
regulate, and control such Libraries, Art Galleries, and Museums,
and shall make Rules and Regulations for the Safety and Use of
the same, and shall also have Power to appoint salaried Officers
and Servants, to pay aud dismiss them, and from Time to Time
to provide the necessary Fuel, Lighting, and other Matters.

Meetings and Chairman of Committee.   XV. The Committee appointed as aforesaid shall in the Case
of a Burgh or District, meet once in every Three Months, or
oftener if necessary, and in the Case of a Parish as often as may
be necessary, to determine as to any Business connected with such
Libraries, Art Galleries, or Museums ; and in the Case of a
Burgh the Provost, in the Case of a District the senior Magistrate, and in the case of a Parish the Chairman of the Parochial
Board, shall be Chairman of such Committee, and such Chairman
shall, in the case of an Equality of Votes, have a Casting Vote
in addition to his Vote as an Individual ; but in the Absence of
such Chairman, the Meeting shall elect a Chairman who, for the
Time being, shall exercise the Privileges of the Chairman appointed under this Act.

When Meeting determine against adoption of Act.   XVI. If any Meeting called as aforesaid to determine as to
the Adoption of this Act for any Burgh, District, or Parish shall
determine against the Adoption, no Meeting for a similar Purpose
shall be held for the Space of Two Years at least from the Time
of holding the previous Meeting.

Art Galleries or Museums may be added.   XVII. Wherever a Public Library has been established under
any Acts relating to Public Libraries or Museums, or shall here-
after be established under this Act, an Art Gallery or Museum,.
as the case may be, may at any Time be established in connection therewith, without any further Proceedings being taken
under this Act.

Libraries, &c., to be free.   XVIII. All Libraries, Art Galleries, or Museums established.
under this Act shall be open to the Public free of all Charge.

XIX. In citing this Act for any Purpose whatever it shall be sufficient to use the Expression "The Public Libraries Act (*Scotland*), 1867." Short Title.

PUBLIC LIBRARIES ACT (SCOTLAND, 1867) AMENDMENT ACT, 1871.

34 AND 35 VICTORIA, CAP. LIX.

An Act to amend "The Public Libraries (*Scotland*) Act, 1867," and to give additional facilities to the Local Authorities entrusted with carrying the same into execution.

[31st July, 1871.]

'WHEREAS it is expedient to amend "The Public Libraries Act (*Scotland*), 1867." and to give additional facilities and powers to the local authorities entrusted with the control, management, and regulation of libraries, museums, and art galleries established under the powers and provisions of said Act, in order to render such libraries, museums, and art galleries of greater utility :' Be it therefore enacted by the Queen's most Excellent Majesty, by and with the advice and consent of the Lords Spiritual and Temporal, and Commons, in the present Parliament assembled, and by the authority of the same, as follows :

I. Sections seven and eight of the said "Public Libraries Act (*Scotland*), 1867, are hereby repealed. 30 and 31 Vict. c. 37, ss. 7, 8, repealed.

II. The "Commissioners' Clauses Act, 1847," with respect to the following matters, that is to say, with respect to the liabilities of the Commissioners, and to legal proceedings by or against the Commissioners, and with respect to mortgages to be executed by the Commissioners, excepting sections eighty-four, eighty-six, and eighty-seven, shall except where expressly varied by this Act, be incorporated with this Act. Parts of 10 and 11 Vict. c. 16, incorporated.

III. The several words and expressions to which by the "Commissioners Clauses Act, 1847," partially incorporated with this Act, meanings are assigned, shall in this Act have the same respective meaning, unless there be something in the subject or context repugnant to such construction : provided always, that in the last-recited Act the expression "the special Act" shall mean the first-recited Act and this Act, and the expression the Commissioners shall mean and include the magistrates and council in the case of a burgh, and the board in the case of a Interpretation of Terms.

parish or district, and the committee appointed in terms of the first-recited Act, in discharge of their respective duties under the said first-recited Act and this Act. Section three of the Public Libraries Act (*Scotland*), 1867, shall be read as if the words "provost, or in his absence the senior magistrate for the time being" were inserted instead of "chief or senior magistrate."

Powers of Borrowing Limited.

IV. The magistrates and council or the board, as the case may be, may, from time to time, borrow at interest on mortgage or bond, on the security of the rates to be levied in pursuance of the first-recited Act and this Act for the purposes thereof, a sum or sums of money not exceeding the capital sum represented by one-fourth part of the library rate of one penny per pound authorized by the first-recited Act capitalized at the rate of twenty years purchase of such sum.

Sinking Fund.

V. The magistrates and council or the board, as the case may be, are hereby required to set apart annually, as a sinking fund for the extinction of capital sums borrowed under the authority of this Act and the said first-recited Act, a sum equal to at least one-fiftieth part of the money so borrowed, and such sinking fund shall be from time to time applied for the redemption of mortgages created under the authority of this Act, and to no other purpose whatever, and shall be lodged in any of the banks in Scotland incorporated by Act of Parliament or Royal Charter, or invested in Government Securities, or lent out at interest in the name and at the discretion of the magistrates and council or the board, as the case may be, until the same be applied for the purposes before specified.

Estimates to be made up.

VI. The committee shall, in the month of April in every year, make up, or cause to be made up, an estimate of the sums required in order to defray the interest of any money borrowed, the payment of the sinking fund, and the expense of maintaining and managing all libraries, art galleries, or museums under their control, for the year after Whitsunday then next to come, and for the purpose of purchasing the articles or thing authorized to be purchased by the first-recited Act, for such libraries, art galleries, or museums, and shall report the same to the magistrates and council in the case of a burgh, or to the board in the case of a parish, for their consideration and approval.

Annual Expenditure to be raised by Assessment not exceeding One Penny per Pound.

VII. The magistrates and council or board, as the case may be, are hereby empowered and required to levy and assess for the purposes of the first-recited Act and this Act a rate not exceeding the sum of one penny in the pound of the yearly rental of such burgh or district, to cover the sum necessary for the purpose of defraying the interest of any money borrowed, and the payment of the sinking fund, together with such sum or sums as they shall fix as the proper and necessary expenses of maintaining and managing all such libraries, art galleries, or museums ; and the magistrates and council or board, as the case may be, are also hereby empowered to levy and assess such sum as may be necessary for the purchase of the articles or things authorized to be purchased by the first-recited Act for such libraries, art galleries, or museums : provided always, that the rates so to be levied and assessed shall not exceed the rate authorized by the first-recited Act.

VIII. The magistrates and council in the case of a burgh, and the board in the case of a district, shall cause the accounts of their receipts, payments, and liabilities with reference to the execution of the first-recited Act and this Act to be annually audited by one or more competent auditors not being members of the committee, and which yearly accounts, as soon as the same shall have been audited, shall be signed by two of the magistrates and council or two members of the board, as the case may be, and shall be printed, and inserted in one or more newspapers published or circulated in the burgh or district. *Accounts to be audited and published annually.*

IX. It shall be lawful for the committee, subject to the approval of the magistrates and council or board, as the case may be, to make bye-laws for regulating all or any matters and things whatsoever connected with the control, management, protection, and use of any property, article, or things vested in them or under their control, for the purposes of the first-recited Act or this Act, and to impose such penalties for breaches of such bye-laws, not exceeding five pounds for each offence, as may be considered expedient ; and from time to time, as they shall think fit, to repeal, alter, vary, or re-enact any such bye-laws : provided always, that such bye-laws shall not be repugnant to the law of Scotland, and before being acted on shall be signed by a quorum of the committee, and approved of by the magistrates, council, or the board ; and approved of and confirmed by the sheriff, and inserted weekly, for at least two weeks, in a newspaper published or circulated in the district ; and all bye-laws so made, signed, approved of, confirmed, and published shall be observed by and binding on all parties concerned therein : provided also, that such bye-laws shall be so framed as to allow the judge before whom any penalty imposed thereby may be sought to be recovered to order a part only of such penalty to be paid, if such judge shall think fit : provided always, that nothing *Power to make Bye-Laws.*

herein contained shall preclude the magistrates and town council or board, as the case may be, from recovering the value of articles or things damaged, or the amount of the damage sustained, against all parties liable for the same.

Penalties and Forfeitures to be recovered by Action. X. All penalties and forfeitures exigible under this Act, and the Acts incorporated wholly or partially herewith, or under any bye-law made in pursuance thereof, may be recovered by an ordinary small debt action in the name of the clerk to the committee for the time being, before either the sheriff or justices of the district, and the same shall be payable to the committee, and shall, when recovered, be applied by them for the purposes of this Act, and in any prosecution under this Act an excerpt from the books of the library committee, certified by the librarian or other proper officer, shall be held equivalent to the books of the library committee, and all entries in the books of the library committee, bearing that any book or books mentioned or referred to therein has or have been borrowed by the person complained against, shall be taken and received as evidence of the fact, and the *onus probandi* shall be thrown on the party complained against, and, if decree passes against said party, he shall be found liable in costs.

Actions to be brought in the Name of the Clerk of the Committee. XI. All actions at the instance of the committee shall be brought in name of the clerk of committee, and in all actions against the committee it shall be sufficient to call the clerk to the committee for the time being as defender, and service on him shall be sufficient service, and all actions brought by or against the clerk to the committee in his official character shall be continued by or against his successors in office without any action of transference.

Mode of supplying Vacancies in the Committee in Case of Resignation, Death, or Disability. XII. In the event of any vacancy occurring in the committee during their term of office by the resignation of any member of committee, the magistrates and council or board, as the case may be, may, at a meeting thereafter, elect a member of committee in place of the member so resigning, provided always that such member so resigning shall give at least fourteen days previous notice of his intention so to resign to the clerk, and in the event of any vacancy occurring in the committee during their term of office by the disability or death of any member of committee, the committee shall intimate the same to the town clerk or clerk to the board, and the magistrate and council or the board, as the case may be, may, at a meeting thereafter, elect a member of committee in room and place of the member of committee who may have become disqualified or died ; Provided always, that no proceeding of the Committee shall be invalidated or be illegal in consequence of there being any vacancy in the number of Committee.

XIII. It shall be lawful for the Committee, and they are hereby authorized and empowered, to lend out for the purpose of being read by the inhabitants of the district or burgh for which they are constituted the Books in the Library, or which may be purchased for the Library, or any such of them as they may consider proper. *Power to lend out Books.*

XIV. The Committee may compile and print catalogues of all articles and things in the Libraries, Art Galleries, or Museums, under their charge, and Reports of their proceedings and sell the same, the proceeds to be applied for the purposes of this Act. *Power to make and issue Catalogues.*

XV. The Committee may lend Books for the use of the inmates of Industrial Schools, Training Ships, Reformatories, Barracks, and other similar institutions established for or in the district for which the Library may be constituted. *Power to issue Books to certain Institutions.*

XVI. This Act may be cited as "The Public Libraries Act (Scotland, 1867,) Amendment Act, 1871." *Short Title.*

PUBLIC LIBRARIES ACT (1855) AMENDMENT ACT, 1871 [ENGLAND].

34 & 35 VICTORIA, CAP. LXXI.

An Act to amend the "Public Libraries Act, 1855."

[14 *August*, 1871.]

WHEREAS it is expedient to amend and extend the Public Libraries Act, 1855, hereinafter referred to as the "principal Act :" *18 and 19 Vict. c. 70.*

Be it therefore enacted by the Queen's most Excellent Majesty, by and with the advice and consent of the Lords Spiritual and Temporal, and Commons, in this present Parliament assembled, and by the authority of the same, as follows :

I. Every Local Board, under the Public Health Act, 1848, and the Local Government Act, 1858, or either of them, is empowered, in like manner as a board under any Improvement Act, to adopt and carry into execution the principal Act. *Local Boards to put principal Act into execution.*

II. For the purposes aforesaid, the following words in the principal Act shall have the following extended significations ; viz., the word "board" shall mean any such local board as aforesaid ; the words "improvement rate" shall mean the general district rate levied by any such board ; the word "ratepayers" *Interpretation of Terms.*

shall mean all persons assessed to and paying such general district rate ; the word " district " shall mean the district in which such local board has any authority to levy a general district rate ; the term "Improvement Act" shall mean the Local Government Act, 1858.

Sec. 15 of recited Act not to apply to Rates made by Local Boards.

III. So much of Section fifteen of the principal Act as refers to the Towns Improvement Clauses Act, 1847, shall not apply to rates made by local boards under the principal Act ; but nothing herein contained shall enable local boards to levy or expend for the purposes of the principal Act any greater sum in any year than one penny in the pound.

Provision as to Borrowing by Local Boards for Purposes of recited Act.

IV. For carrying into execution the principal Act, every such local board may borrow upon mortage of the general district rate, or any separate rate, to be levied under the principal Act ; and such borrowing shall be effected in conformity with the provisions as to borrowing contained in the Local Government Act, 1858, and the Acts incorporated therewith, in lieu of the provisions as to borrowing contained in the principal Act.

Not to apply to certain Districts.

V. This Act shall not apply to any district the whole or any part of which is within any municipal borough, or within the jurisdiction of commissioners under any Improvement Act.

Short Title.

VI. This Act may be cited for all purposes as "The Public Libraries Act, 1855, Amendment Act, 1871."

PUBLIC LIBRARIES ACT (1871): AMENDMENT ACT 1877 [ENGLAND, SCOTLAND, AND IRELAND].

40 AND 41 VICTORIA, CAP. 54.

An Act to amend the "Public Libraries Acts." [14th August, 1877.]

WHEREAS by the Public Libraries Acts, 18 and 19 Victoria, c. 40, for Ireland ; 29 and 30 Victoria, c. 114, for England ; and 30 and 31 Victoria, c. 37, for Scotland, the mode by which the Act is to be adopted is prescribed to be by public meeting, and it has been found that in many cases a public meeting is a most incorrect and unsatisfactory mode, and fails to indicate the general opinion of the ratepayers, and it is desirable to ascertain these opinions more correctly :

Be it enacted by the Queen's most Excellent Majesty, by and with the advice and consent of the Lords Spiritual and Temporal, and Commons, in this present Parliament assembled, and by the authority of the same, as follows:

1. It shall be competent for the prescribed local authority in any place or community which has the power to adopt one of the above recited Acts, to ascertain the opinions of the majority of the ratepayers either by the prescribed public meeting or by the issue of a voting paper to each ratepayer, and the subsequent collection and scrutiny thereof, and any expense in connexion with such voting papers shall be borne in the same way as the expense of a public meeting would be borne, and the decision of the majority so ascertained shall be equally binding. *Ratepayers Opinions may be ascertained by Voting Papers.*

2. In addition to the simple vote "Yes" or "No" to the adoption of the Act, such voting paper may stipulate that its adoption shall be subject to a limitation to some lower rate of assessment than the maximum allowed by Act of Parliament in force at the time, and such lower limit, if once adopted, shall not be subsequently altered except by public vote similarly taken. *Ratepayers may stipulate for modified Assessment.*

3. "Ratepayer" shall mean every inhabitant who would have to pay the Free Library assessment in event of the Act being adopted. *Definition.*

4. This Act may be cited as "The Public Libraries Amendment Act, 1877." *Short Title.*

MALICIOUS INJURIES TO PROPERTY ACT (1861) [ENGLAND AND IRELAND],

24TH AND 25TH VICTORIA, CAP. 97, § 39.

WHOEVER shall unlawfully and maliciously destroy or damage any Book, Manuscript, Picture, Print, Statue, Bust or Vase, or any other Article or Thing kept for the purposes of Art, Science, or Literature, or as an Object of Curiosity, in any Museum, Gallery, Cabinet, Library, or other Repository, which Museum, Gallery, Cabinet, Library, or other Repository is either at all Times or from Time to Time open for the Admission of the Public or of any considerable Number of Persons to view the same, either by the Permission of the Proprietor thereof or by the Payment of Money before entering the same, or any Picture, Statue, Monument, or other Memorial of the Dead, Painted Glass, or other Ornament or Work of Art, in any Church, Chapel, Meeting House, or other Place of Divine Worship, or in any Building belonging to the Queen, or to any County, Riding, Division, City, Borough, Poor-Law Union, Parish, or Place, or to any University, or College or Hall of any University, or to any Inn of Court, or in any Street, Square, Churchyard, Burial Ground, Public Garden or Ground, or any Statue or Monument exposed to Public View, or any Ornament, Railing, or Fence surrounding such Statue or Monument, shall be guilty of a Misdemeanour, and being convicted thereof, shall be liable to be imprisoned for any Term not exceeding Six Months, with or without Hard Labour, and, if a Male under the Age of Sixteen Years, with or without Whipping : provided, that nothing herein contained shall be deemed to affect the Right of any Person to recover, by Action at Law, Damages for the Injury so committed.

APPENDIX II.

RULES AND REGULATIONS SUITABLE FOR FREE LIBRARIES,

With Forms in Use, etc.

FREE LENDING LIBRARIES.

RULES AND REGULATIONS.

1. The Chief Librarian shall have the general charge of the Libraries, and shall be responsible for the safe keeping of the books, and of all other property belonging thereto.

2. The Newsrooms shall be open to the Public, every day (Sundays, Christmas Day, and Good Friday excepted), from Nine o'clock a.m., to Ten o'clock p.m., and the Library from Ten o'clock a.m., to Nine o'clock p.m.

3. No person shall be admitted who is in a state of intoxication ; nor shall any audible conversation be permitted in the Rooms ; nor shall any person be allowed to partake of refresh-

ments therein. Any person who shall offend against these regulations, or shall be guilty of any misconduct, shall not be allowed to remain within the building.

4. No person shall be allowed to pass within the enclosure of the Libraries, or to take any book from the shelves, except by permission of the Librarian.

5. Persons enrolled as Burgesses of the Borough of shall be entitled to borrow books on their own responsibility. Persons not so enrolled shall be required to obtain the signature of one Burgess to the following voucher, which must be renewed annually :

"I, the undersigned, being a Burgess of the Borough of , declare that I believe
Occupation age of No.
to be a person to whom books may be safely entrusted for perusal; and I hereby undertake to replace or to pay the value of any book, belonging to the Corporation of , which shall be lost or materially injured by the said Borrower."

Any person having signed this engagement, who shall afterwards desire to withdraw from the same, must give notice thereof in writing to the Librarian, who will give a release as soon as he shall have ascertained that no loss has been incurred.

This voucher must be delivered to the Librarian three days before the first issue of books to the person recommended.

6. All books borrowed must be returned to the Libraries within the time specified on the respective covers, under a penalty of one penny for the whole or any portion of the first week, and one penny for each week or portion of a week afterwards.

7. The Librarian shall carefully examine, or cause to be examined, each book returned, and if the same be found to have sustained any injury or damage, he shall require the person to whom the same was delivered, or his guarantor, to pay the amount of damage or injury done, or otherwise to procure a new copy of the book of equal value, and in the latter case such person shall be entitled to the damaged copy on depositing the new one.

8. All books borrowed from the Libraries must be returned, irrespective of the time allowed for reading, at the half-yearly dates specified on the printed labels at the beginning of each book ; Borrowers neglecting to comply with this regulation will risk the forfeiture of their privilege of borrowing books.

9. Borrowers leaving town, or ceasing to use the Libraries,

are requested to return their tickets to the Librarian, in order to have them cancelled, otherwise they and their guarantors will be held responsible for any book taken out in their names.

10. Borrowers, when they change their residence, are required to hand in their ticket with their present address to the Librarian, otherwise they will lose their right of borrowing books.

11. Borrowers are cautioned against losing their tickets, as they will be held responsible for any book or books that may be taken out of the Libraries in their names.

12. No Borrower will be allowed to have more than one work at the same time.

13. No book can be renewed more than once, if required by another Borrower.

14. No Borrower will be allowed to make use of more than one of the Lending Libraries at the same time.

15. The Librarian shall have the power to refuse Books to any Borrower who shall neglect to comply with the Rules and Regulations of the Library; but any person so refused shall have liberty to appeal to the Library Committee.

16. That the Free Libraries Committee shall not make any dividend, gift, division, or bonus in money, unto or between any of its members.

By order.

Librarian.

RULES AND REGULATIONS

OF THE

REFERENCE LIBRARY.

No person will be allowed to obtain any Book without signing a Reader's Ticket," and such signature shall be taken and considered to be an assent to the Rules and Regulations of the Library.

Readers giving a false name and address will be held responsible for the consequences.

Readers cannot obtain more than one work on the same Ticket.

It is expressly forbidden to take out of the Reading Room any Book, Map, Manuscript, or other article belonging to the Library, or to write or make any marks upon the same.

Readers desirous of proposing Books for addition to the Library, or of making any suggestion as to its management, may do so by writing the same in a Suggestion Book, which is regularly submitted to the Committee for consideration.

No person will be admitted to the Library who is intoxicated, or in a dirty condition ; nor will any conversation be permitted in the room.

No person is allowed to pass within the enclosure, except by special permission of the Librarian.

Persons under fourteen years of age are not admitted to the Reference Library, except for special purposes to be determined by the Librarian.

The costly Illustrated Works are issued only on written application to the Committee.

Newspapers having been cut, and Illustrated Works disfigured, are in future to be used on the large round Tables near the Desk. Copying is permitted, but not tracing, as this has resulted in damage to the Illustrations. Readers are particularly requested not to soil or injure the Illustrations by fingering or laying their hands on them.

The use of Ink for copying extracts, etc., is not permitted, as serious injury to Plates and Books has resulted therefrom.

FORM OF VOUCHER FOR GENERAL PUBLIC.

Books can be had out only by Persons Rated for, Resident in, or Employed in the Borough.

This Voucher must be signed by a Burgess who is enrolled on the Burgess List of the Borough of _____. Inattention to this regulation will cause trouble and disappointment.

By Order,
_____, Chief Librarian.

FREE LIBRARIES.

I, the undersigned, being a Burgess of the Borough of _____, occupation _____, declare that I believe

_____ of No. _____ aged _____ occupation _____ to be a person to whom Books may be safely entrusted for perusal; and I hereby undertake to replace or pay the value of any Book belonging to the CORPORATION OF _____, which shall be lost or materially injured by the said Borrower.

GUARANTOR'S NAME.	OCCUPATION.	ADDRESS.	WARD.

Dated this _____ day of _____, 1868.

The Library is open for the issue and return of Books daily, between the hours of TEN in the Morning and NINE in the Evening, uninterruptedly.

Vouchers in due form, are received at the Library at any time between the hours of TEN in the Morning, and NINE in the Evening; and if on examination they be found correct, Tickets will be issued on the FOURTH DAY after the Receipt of the Vouchers.

SPECIAL NOTICE.—Borrowers are cautioned against losing their Ticket, as they and the Guarantors will be held responsible for any Book that may be taken out with such Ticket.

When the person who has signed this engagement shall desire to withdraw from it, he must give notice "thereof in writing to the Librarian, who will give a release as soon as he shall have ascertained that no liability has been incurred!"

No._____

FORM OF VOUCHER FOR BURGESSES.

FREE LIBRARIES.

LENDING LIBRARY,

I, the undersigned, being a Burgess of the Borough of ———, hereby make application to the Free Libraries Committee for A BORROWER'S TICKET, entitling me to borrow Books from LENDING LIBRARY; and I undertake to be responsible for any loss the CORPORATION OF may sustain by loss or damage of any Book in my possession.

Signed, ———

NAME OF APPLICANT.	ADDRESS OF APPLICANT.	OCCUPATION OF APPLICANT.

Personal Application must be made for the Ticket.

No. ———

BORROWER'S CARD. *Front.*

Free Libraries.

Branch (or Central) Library

Not Transferable.

No.———

The Bearer————————————

of——————————————————

is entitled to borrow Books.

Chief Librarian.

————, 187 .

BORROWER'S CARD. *Back.*

Free Libraries.

REGULATIONS OF THE LENDING DEPARTMENT.

No Book can be issued without the presentation of this Ticket.

Books lost or injured, while in the possession of Borrowers, must be replaced, or the amount chargeable for their loss or injury, must be paid by the Borrowers or their Guarantors.

Borrowers detaining Books beyond the time allowed for reading, will be fined One Penny for the whole or any portion of the first week, and One Penny for each week or portion of a week afterwards.

All Books borrowed from the Library must be returned on or before the LAST TUESDAY IN JUNE AND DECEMBER respectively, on pain of losing the privilege of borrowing in future.

Any person returning a Book without taking out another at the same time, must leave the Library Ticket with the Librarian until another Book is taken.

The Lending Departments are open for the delivery and return of Books from TEN o'clock in the Morning until NINE o'clock in the Evening.

By order,

Chief Librarian.

REFERENCE LIBRARY.

BOOK RETURNED.

Title

Recd. by

Date

REFERENCE LIBRARY.—READER'S TICKET.

FREE LIBRARY.—REFERENCE DEPARTMENT.—READER'S TICKET.

	Attended to by
The Reader must write upon this Form the Title of the Book which he requires, as described in the Catalogue, together with his Signature, Address, Age, and Profession. The Catalogues must not be removed from the Tables upon which they lie. Further information may be obtained upon application to the Librarian. Every Reader, before leaving the room, must return the Book delivered to him, in exchange for which he will receive the annexed Receipt.	
Title, etc., of Book requested	Replaced by
READER'S { Signature Address Age Profession } N.B.—The Reader's Age and Profession are desired for the purpose of Statistical Information.	
Ticket's Date, 187	

APPENDIX III.

COPY OF REQUISITION.

To the Chairman and Members of the Local Board of Health.

Whereas by an Act of Parliament passed in the 18th and 19th years of Queen Victoria, chapter 70, intituled "The Public Libraries Act, 1855," which Act was amended by another Act passed in the 29th and 30th years of the reign of Queen Victoria, chapter 114, intituled "The Public Libraries Amendment Act, 1866," it is provided that "The Board of any District being a place within the limits of any Improvement Act, shall, upon the Requisition in writing of at least ten persons assessed to, and paying the Improvement Rate, appoint a time not less than ten days nor more than twenty days from the time of receiving such Requisition for a Public Meeting of the persons assessed to and paying such Rate, in order to determine whether these Acts shall be adopted for such District.

We, the undersigned, being persons assessed to and paying Rates to the Local Board of Health for the District or Township of   , do hereby respectfully request you to call a Meeting of Persons assessed to and paying Rates to your Board, for the purpose of determining whether or not the above-mentioned Acts shall be adopted for such District, in manner provided by the said Acts.

APPENDIX IV.

Copy of Resolution passed at a Meeting of Rate-payers held on the 26th December, 1876.

"Proposed by Mr.   , and seconded by Mr.   , that 'The Public Libraries Act, 1855,' be adopted for the District of   , in the County of   , in pursuance of the Acts of Parliament in that behalf."

APPENDIX V.

BOOKS FOR A FREE LENDING LIBRARY, RANGING IN PRICE FROM 1s TO 7s 6d PER VOL.

This list is not made upon any Theory of what Books people ought to read, but from experience of which they will read. It is also intended to refer to one volume editions of the works named, as editions in numerous volumes are found to be wasteful and inconvenient for Lending Libraries, though very suitable for the Reference Department.

Selections from Bohn's Antiquarian, Ecclesiastical, Historical and Standard Libraries, over 100 vols.

CONSTABLE'S MISCELLANY, containing Literature, Science and Arts, History, Voyages and Travels, etc., 82 vols.

EDINBURGH CABINET LIBRARY, containing History, Geography, Topography, Voyages, etc., 38 vols.

JARDINE'S NATURALIST'S LIBRARY (Illustrated), 40 vols.

LARDNER'S CABINET CYCLOPÆDIA, containing History, Biography, Literature, Arts and Sciences, Natural History and Manufactures, etc., 132 vols.

Low's Standard Library of Travel and Adventure, 10 or more vols. at 7s 6d

LIBRARY OF ENTERTAINING KNOWLEDGE, containing Antiquities, History, Natural History, Topography, Trials, etc., 43 vols.

MURRAY'S FAMILY LIBRARY, containing History, Biography, Natural History, Science, Voyages and Travels, etc., 80 vols.

WEALE'S RUDIMENTARIES : comprising Science, History, Languages, Grammar, etc.

Over 100 vols. from 1s to 2s per volume.

TRAVELLER'S LIBRARY, containing History, Biography, Voyages, Travels, Essays, 25 vols.

CONDER'S MODERN TRAVELLER, 30 vols.

PERCY ANECDOTES, 20 vols.

THEOLOGY, MORAL PHILOSOPHY, ETC. Barnes's Notes on the Scriptures ; Bible Handbook by Angus ; Analogy of Religion by Butler ; " Ecce Homo ;" Paley's Evidences ; Bacon's

Essays ; Lectures published by the Christian Evidence
Society, special and popular volumes by Alford, Arnold,
Arnot, Bunyan, Beecher, Binney, Caird, Cheever, R. W.
Dale, Goulburn, Guthrie, Hamilton, Hanna, Helps, Kings-
ley, Landels, MacDonald, MacLeod, Mursell, Newman,
Spurgeon ; Trench on the Miracles and Parables ; Sermons,
etc. by F. W. Robertson, A. P. Stanley, Talmage, Vaughan,
and John Wesley.

Browne on the Thirty-nine Articles ; Cook's Boston Lectures,
Biblical Reason Why; Congregational Lectures by Davidson,
Halley, Hamilton, Stowell, Vaughan, Wardlaw, etc., 15 vols.

Clark's Foreign Theological Library, in numerous vols.; smaller
Edition of Smith's Dictionary of the Bible, Conybeare
and Howson's St. Paul.

Logic by Mill, and Logic and Rhetoric by Whately.

GEOGRAPHY. Physical Geography by Ansted ; Geography by
Hughes ; Student's Modern Geography by Bevan ; Beeton's
Gazetteers.

HISTORY, ETC. Allen's Battles of the British Army ; Fifteen
Decisive Battles of the World by Creasy ; Jewish War by
Josephus ; Great Battles of the British Army ; Napier's
Peninsular War ; Gleig's Waterloo ; the Victoria History
of England ; the Student's Hume ; History of England
and History of France by J. White ; Green's Short History
of the English People ; Manual of English History by
Ross ; History of England by Macaulay ; Carlyle's French
Revolution ; Irish Rebellion by Maxwell ; Greater Britain
by Dilke ; Rise of the Dutch Republic by Motley ;
Cassell's History of the Franco-German War ; Greece
by Smith ; Rome by Gibbon, Liddell and Merivale,
(Student's Editions); White's Northumberland and the
Border, his Month in Yorkshire, and All Round the
Wrekin ; Kohl's America ; New America by Dixon ;
Africa by Gordon Cumming, Baker, Burton, Du Chaillu,
Moffatt, and Livingstone ; Stanley's How I found Living-
stone ; Rob Roy Voyages by MacGregor ; Russell's Diary
in India; America, North and South ; The Crimean War
by Chambers and Russell ; The Switzers by Dixon ; Arctic
Voyages by Dufferin, Hooper, and McClintock ; Knights
of the Frozen Sea ; Layard's Nineveh ; Epitome of Alison's
Europe ; Student's Hallam ; Voyages of Captain Cook ;
Mungo Park ; Boy's Voyage Round the World by Smiles ;
Abyssinia by Parkyns ; Dutch at Home by Esquiros ;

Australia by Howitt, Kennedy, Lang, Harcus and Sidney; Canada by Grant, Russell and Marshall; Letters on England by Esquiros and Louis Blanc; Eighteen Christian Centuries by White; India by Capper, Hodson and Ludlow; Italy by Manning and Vieusseux; Ride to Khiva by Burnaby; London by Archer, Burritt, Grant, Greenwood, Leigh Hunt and Timbs; Mexico by Ruxton; New Zealand by Kennedy and Lady Barker; Norway by Williams; Russia by Kohl and Edwards; Scotland by Miller and Ramsay; Turkey by Creasy and Freeman.

BIOGRAPHY.—Life of Byron, Burns, Dickens, Lamartine's Celebrated Characters, Nelson, Wesley, Anne Boleyn, Mary Queen of Scots, Marie Antoinette, Sir W. Scott, Stricklands' Lives of the Queens of England, Life of Johnson by Boswell, Life of Wellington by Maxwell, Boyhood of Great Men, Life of Cromwell by Carlyle, Smiles' Self-Help and Character, Industrial Biography, Lives of Engineers by Smiles, Mayhew's London Labour and London Poor, Boyhood of Great Men, Our Exemplars—Men who have Risen; Lives of King Alfred, Prince Albert, Arnold by Stanley, Lord Bacon by Dixon, Epoch Men by Neil; Beeton's British Biography, Great Men by Myers, Actors by Russell, Admirals by Campbell or Tytler, Neptune's Heroes by Adams, Female Artists and Queens of Song by Clayton, Queens of Society and Wits and Beauties by Wharton; Biographies by Macaulay, Page, Miss Martineau, and Maunder; Eminent Soldiers by Mitchell, Representative Men by Emerson.

NATURAL HISTORY by Beeton, Buckland, Buffon (Abridged), Gosse, and Jesse; Phrenology by Combe, Smaller Edition of Natural History by Wood, Botany by Balfour, Bentley, and Oliver, Bechstein's Birds, Physiology of Common Life by Lewes.

KING'S INTERNATIONAL SCIENTIFIC SERIES, containing works by Bagehot, Bain, Cooke, Tyndall, Vogel, etc., 20 to 30 vols. at 4s and 5s.

TEXT BOOKS OF SCIENCE.—Chemistry, etc., etc., by Bloxam, Bowman, Frankland, Goodeve, Gore, Griffin, Johnston, Liebig, Maxwell, Miller, Odling, Thorpe, etc.

SCIENCE PRIMERS and Class Books by Airy, Geikie, Huxley, Jevons, Roscoe, etc., issued by Macmillan at 1s to 3s 6d.

Electricity by Faraday, Ferguson, Buckmaster, Tyndall; Electric Telegraph by Lardner; Lankester's Lectures on Food; Music by Hullah, Turle, Taylor, Spencer, etc.; Astronomy by Airey, Herschel, Lockyer and Proctor; Orr's Circle of the Sciences; Geology by Ansted, Geikie, Jukes, Kingsley, Lyell, Miller, Page, and Ramsay; Works on Heat, Light, and Sound, by Tyndall, Proctor, and Buckmaster; Gardening by Beeton, Glenny, Hibberd, and Loudon; The Useful Metals and their Alloys; Metallurgy by Gore and Phillips.

BRITISH MANUFACTURING INDUSTRIES, edited by Bevan, 10 or more vols. at 3s 6d.

Arithmetic and Algebra by Colenso, Haddon, Barnard Smith, and Todhunter.

The Steam Engine and Engineering by Bourne, Fairbairn, Rankine, and Tredgold.

Photography by Hunt, Sutton, and Abney.

Phonography by Pitman and others.

Heraldry by Boutell.

Printing. Johnson's Typographia, and Knight's Old Printer and Modern Press.

" Things not generally known" and similar books by Timbs.

POLITICAL ECONOMY by Fawcett, J. S. Mill, and Adam Smith. Mill on Liberty; Speeches by Bright, Disraeli, Gladstone, Lowe; the English Constitution by Brougham, Creasy, and Earl Russell; Representative Government by Mill; Best Form of Government by Cornewall Lewis; Levi on Taxation.

NICHOL'S ENGLISH POETS, comprising Chaucer, Milton, Spenser, Cowper, Burns, Akenside, etc., 42 vols.

ALDINE SERIES OF ENGLISH POETS.

Johnson's Lives and Works of the British Poets.

CHANDOS CLASSICS. Poetry, History and General Literature, containing Shakespeare, Burns, Byron, Scott, Eliza Cook, Pope, Arabian Nights, etc., etc., 48 vols. 2s each.

SELECTIONS FROM MODERN POETS. Browning, Buchanan, Lytton, Longfellow, Lowell, Mackay, Poe, Tennyson, Whittier, Wordsworth.

Selections from the Dramatists.

FICTION.

BENTLEY'S NOVELS; about 50 vols. at 6s each.

STANDARD LIBRARY (Hurst and Blackett).

SELECT LIBRARY OF FICTION, containing 120 to 130 vols. at about 2s 6d each.

Routledge's Railway Library, about 600 vols. at 1s and 2s each.

Such of the following Authors as are not sufficiently represented in the above sets :—Aguilar, Aimard, Ainsworth, Allcott, Austen, Black, Blackmore, Braddon, Armstrong, Besant and Rice, Bowman, Ballantyne, Brontë, Disraeli, Collins, Cooper, Dickens, Eliot, Gaskell, Holmes, Hughes, James, Lever, Lytton, Macdonald, Kingsley, Marryat, Melville, Mulock, Charles Reade, Mayne Reid, Sala, Scott, Stowe, Thackeray, Trollope, Wilson (Tales of the Borders), Warren, Worboise, Wood, Yonge, Erckmann-Chatrian, Farjeon, Grant, Hugo, Kingston, Manning, Maxwell, Oliphant, Robinson, Sewell, Tales from Blackwood, 20 vols. Tales from Bentley, 10 vols.

MISCELLANEOUS.

Ancient Classics, Introductions to, Æschylus, Aristotle, Aristophanes, Cæsar, Cicero, Euripides, Herodotus, Hesiod, Homer, Horace, Juvenal, Lucian, Plato, Plautus and Terence, Pliny's Letters, Sophocles, Tacitus, Virgil, Zenophon, 20 to 30 vols. at 2s 6d each.

Half-Hours with the Best Authors, Essays by Carlyle, Essays by Emerson, by Macaulay, British Essayists, Arnold's Manual of English Literature, the British Controversialist, 30 vols., Burritt's Sparks from the Anvil, etc., etc., Chambers's Miscellany, Chambers's Papers for the People.

PERIODICALS.

For these the demand in most libraries is very urgent. They may be bought, bound strongly, for from 3s to 5s the volume.

All the Year Round, Argosy, Belgravia, Cassell's, Chambers's Journal, Cornhill, Good Words, Day of Rest, Household Words, Leisure Hour, Once a Week, Sunday at Home, Sunday Magazine, Temple Bar, Tinsley's.

JUVENILE BOOKS.

See such authors as Abbott, Andersen, Adams, Ballantyne, Howitt, Grimm, Kingston, Hesba Stretton, Mrs. Gatty, Miss Wetherell, Miss Yonge ; Boys' Magazine, Boys' Annuals, Books of Games, Magnet Stories, Pleasant Pages.